BAGGAGE CLAIM

Baggage Claim

PROVIDE, INVEST & EMPOWER: COVENANT INGREDIENTS TO MARRIAGE (2ND EDITION)

Kimberly H. Miller
Newton H. Miller II

newED products publishing

TITLE: Baggage Claim 2nd Edition

By: Kimberly H. Miller and Dr. Newton H. Miller II
Cover: Ommyz World Creations
ISBN-13: 979-8-89292-507-5
Copyright 2023

Permission: For information on getting permission for reprints and excerpts, contact the authors at:

www.newedproducts.net
msap@newedproducts.net

Contents

Acknowledgements

To our earthly sources of life, we honor you for your example and sacrifice. Thank you, Dr. Newton H. Miller Sr., Elaine L. Miller, Otto Sexton, and Patsy J. Coleman. In the journey of life, everyone you encounter deposits something from which you can learn and grow. Those individuals closest to you have no doubt made more deposits that anyone else. We thank our wonderful children Akai, Briante, Tamika, Anthony, Atory, Newton, and Monique. You have been a source of love, inspiration, motivation and encouragement for us. We are honored to be your parents.

Many of our friends have helped shape and edit this book. Lewellyn, Lisa, Victoria, and Candace: we cannot express in words how grateful we are for the time talent and energy you invested in us to complete this work. Mr. Rocky McDonald: thank you for your enthusiasm and creative eye, your photoshoots are amazing. We love all of you.

Finally, there are four individuals that have impacted each of our lives in very powerful ways. We render a special thanks to Dr. Gwendolyn and Charles Matthews, Elder Carl C. White, Apostle Alexander Thompson, and Apostle Ron Carpenter, Jr. You have no idea how much you have helped shape our thinking and character.

Foreward

MAKING LOVE WORK FOR US THE SECOND TIME AROUND

History has a way of reminding us of who we are, and from whence we've come. History consists of many different facets, from the painful memories of death, the beautiful experience of life, and the broadest span in between them both: Love. Love is universal and can be self-satisfying if it encompasses everything you desire within your own personal relationships. Love has no timing. Some say it just happened to them when they least expected it; Love gives no warning. It's been known to be easy to fall into and, for some, just as simple to fall out of. Love is even more promising and beautiful when you can watch its progression. Watch its beauty in summer's bud, change colors in its fall, see it withering in love's winter, just to see it flourish and replenish in love's spring. Love is far beyond a mere feeling. Love in its truest entity is selflessness. This couple, which I had the honor of interviewing, is near and dear to my heart—my oldest sister, Kimberly Miller, and my now big brother, Dr. Newton Miller. I want to share a few tidbits that I collected from that interview to give you a glimpse of their love story from the inside.

Words From Our Sister

After parenting a very busy household of seven, five children plus themselves, they moved across the country to finally have time to enjoy one another. It was almost like they were getting to know each other all over again. When asked if they would do it again, Kim said, "I would really make him work harder, expect him to say more, be forward and honest about everything up front." Newton said, "I would rather that we had received more counseling in our time before saying I do." They both agreed that they would marry each other again, but with more stipulations and higher expectations. I will say I've watched this couple at their best and their worst, and, with that, I agree it takes work. Regardless, work doesn't work without love. You can work all day on something, but if your heart is not in it, it's as good as dead. In comparison to 24 years ago, I see a totally different and mature marriage that can outlast the tests of time. They are committed to doing the work and have developed the kind of determination that brings longevity. I am their number one supporter and fan. Not only am I proud that they have made it this far, but it gives me hope and inspiration to know that it is possible to *make love work, the second time around!!*

Lewellyn Coleman-Hogue

Testimonial

When my dear friend, Newt and his lovely bride Kim, asked me to read their book, I did not expect it to impact me so powerfully. I did not expect it to jerk back the cover and reveal the mess that I have kept hidden for so many years. Like a mirror, Newt and Kim's honest and frank transparency exposed my own negative habits and patterns, causing me to face myself head on.

You see, like the woman at the well (John 4:5-30), I have experienced love and loss, acceptance and rejection, joy and pain. THREE MARRIAGES! Three marriages – and countless other relationships that were dysfunctional, abusive and painful – before I finally found my Boaz, the one my soul loves (Ruth; Song of Solomon 3:1). Yet, if your mind is not renewed and therefore, your life transformed (Romans 12:1-2), inevitably you will revert back to those old habits. I recently started self-sabotaging my beautiful covenant, believing the lies from the enemy of our souls. That is when I started reading "Baggage Claim," and, like a divine intervention, Newt and Kim's real and rough testimony opened my eyes, forced me to pump my brakes, and to decisively make positive changes in my life.

Newt and Kim offer their experience - the good, bad, and ugly - without restraint. But most importantly, they offer the reader HOPE! Wisdom and knowledge flow from this book like a refreshing stream of water. Relevant and relatable, Newt and Kim share their journey, showing us how to make a dysfunctional relationship into a dynamic covenant of unconditional love and mutual respect. If you want to change the direction of your relationship from bad to good to even better, apply the principles in this book. Newt and Kim have done the hard work for us. And I promise you, your life and relationship will forever be changed!

Grateful,
Lisa M. Johnson

Introduction

SIMPLE IS NOT ALWAYS EASY!

Newt's Story

It was a Sunday afternoon at Maranatha Church when I saw this beautiful woman in a black knit dress standing in the front of the church smiling and laughing with two other young ladies. One of the young ladies I knew and later learned was her aunt, and the other, well, I really don't remember her except that she was there when we met. I was minding my own business gathering and organizing the audio equipment. That was my job; I was the sound guy. I didn't ask her name or even act like I noticed her, but I did. I kept on rolling up the microphone wires pretending not to be interested. Finally, as if God was eavesdropping on my thoughts, her aunt called me over to where they were to introduce us. I put down the cords as cool as I could because I didn't want to seem anxious. I stood up straight and walked over with the best Denzel Washington stroll I could muster. We were introduced, and I could tell she wasn't interested in me. Quite frankly, though she was beautiful, I wasn't in any position to be interested in her either. Let me explain.

I had just endured a pretty rough divorce and wasn't looking to get into a serious relationship. But she had this smile that lit up the room and sparkle in her eye that made me feel like everything was going to be alright. So, I was very curious. At the very least, I definitely had room in my life for a friend. In those first few minutes at the front of the church, it was evident she was classy and took pride in making sure that she was perceived as a person of character and substance. But she was also down to earth, treated everyone kindly, and wasn't afraid to laugh. The next thing I knew, I was walking them out of the church. I never did finish rolling up the microphone cords that day.

Although I can clearly recall the encounter, I don't remember any of the conversation other than the introduction. I guess that smile and sparkle were already settling into the soil of my soul distracting me from the present and propelling me to another place and time. However, I do remember that black dress... Whoo wee! It fit so perfectly. Not too tight and provocatively revealing, nor was it too loose and covering her from her earlobes to her ankles. It sent a clear message that I was beholding a great treasure, and that she knew it and expected to be treated like one. The way she looked in that dress made such an impression on me that from time to time over the years I would tease her about the black dress trying to get her to blush in front of the kids. I think everyone in our family knows all about the story of the black dress.

As fate would have it, a friend of mine asked her to join us for Easter dinner at his mother's house. That was my chance to learn a little more about her. But I was playing it cool, especially since I was new to the city, I had my son with me, and I didn't want anyone to know that I was checking her out. A few weeks later, our paths crossed again, I was invited to watch a movie with a group of friends, and there she was again. While talking, I realized that we had a few things in common. She knew about Wagner Alumni and was friends with the director, who I admired. I knew her favorite cousin from my years at Lincoln University where I began my bachelor's degree. Now, I know those things were somewhat unrelated, and it was a stretch to make them fit together as my way of continuing the conversation. I guess it's obvious that we didn't really watch the movie. As a matter of fact, I don't even remember what movie was playing.

About a week later, I saw her again. She was wearing a Tommy Hilfiger skirt set that caught my eye as I came up the stairs from the basement of her aunt's house where I was staying. There she stood helping her aunt, washing dishes, and flashing that signature smile that pierced my heart. I took my time coming up those stairs taking advantage of every possible moment to drink in the sight of her. Clearly, I was excited to see her again, and a little nervous too, because after I knew she saw me, I suddenly got super clumsy and ran into the gate outside. Everyone saw my awkward and embarrassing move. Kim's friend broke the tension by noting that I was distracted. I played it off pretty well; at least, I thought so. Either I was the smooth operator I thought I was, or she took pity on my clumsiness. Either way, she agreed to join me for a water ice, a walk in the park, and dinner. Our hearts were being knit together as we grew closer and all of the moving pieces of our lives seemed to complement well. Four months later, we were planning a wedding. It was fast, but it felt like I knew her all my life, and we learned so much about each other in that short period of time. I often tell her that it was like God set us up—you know, arranging our meeting. The next thing I knew, we were getting married under the gazebo in her uncle's backyard. Come to think of it, I never did pay him back the $35 he gave me to pay for the marriage license. Looking back, it was quite the adventure, in fact our entire time together has been an adventure, and I wouldn't change a thing.

Kim's Story

I remember meeting Newt and instantly having the sense that he was kind, loving, helpful, smart, and fun to be around. He was well-spoken which was funny at first. But after learning more about his background, I thought that it was adorable. After spending time with Newt, I loved everything about him. He treated me like I was fragile. I guess it was because of everything that I shared with him about my previous relationship. Newt was kind and considerate, and we established a great connection.

Newt wanted me beside him everywhere he went in the early days of our relationship. I guess he wanted to make sure I knew how special I was to him. This was a new thing for me, especially after dealing with the difficulties of my first marriage. But, because of the residue of my first marriage, I was suspicious. So, I watched and listened to everything to make sure I could trust Newt. I was pleasantly surprised to see that he didn't have an ulterior motive, neither was he trying to get anything from me. He had children—four of them. I had children as well—three of them. He wanted to be with me and build one unit out of the family we had independent of each other. That was very attractive to me.

As we committed to each other, it became apparent that our backgrounds were quite different. Newt lived with both of his parents, but I grew up in a home with my mother and, for a short time, my stepfather, stepsiblings. On some weekends, I visited my father. So, our understanding of family was different.

Newt had witnessed the longevity of his parents' marriage, so he was dedicated to the work that it would take to ensure that our marriage worked. I was a bit more skeptical because of the failed marriages I had seen in my family and experienced in my own life. Despite our differences, we were on our way to figuring this thing out together. We both believed that if we worked together and kept the three cords of our marriage (the two of us and God) tightly knit together, we would be able to weather every storm. And boy, oh boy, there were storms.

I loved Newt and he loved me, and it was obvious to everyone who came into contact with us. But we needed much more in addition to our love. You see, marriage is Simple, but it's not always easy. One reason is that we, as individuals, have an innate craving to please ourselves and meet our own desires. So, marriage isn't what's difficult–we are! So, in addition to loving each other, we needed tools and skills that would protect that love and ensure our union was a lasting one.

We titled this book "Baggage Claim" because identifying and owning your stuff is an essential step in establishing a healthy marriage relationship. God laid it on our hearts to create the outline of this book together, and then go to our neutral corners and start writing. When we came back together to review what we had written, the only thing we could do was laugh. Our thoughts and message synergized so well, you would think we were in the same room, writing side by side. That being said, we decided to leave the project as is so you can see how similar our paths, but different our processes were as we worked to accomplish the same goal - a strong and healthy marriage relationship.

We believe there are two basic ways to learn life lessons: through a mentor or teacher or to let life itself teach you on its terms. In all transparency, throughout the years, both methods have occurred for us. Although it can be a painful process, we do tend to learn a great deal from our experiences. We don't believe that it is God's desire for any of us to re-travel ground or repeat what others have already shown to be an unpleasant path that brings us pain and loss. Thus, we believe part of our purpose and calling is to help light the path for others, so they don't have to make the same mistakes as those that have travelled a similar road before them.

Before we go any further, we are not marriage counselors. In fact, both of our first marriages failed after six and sixteen years respectively. So, this is our second go around. That being said, we are both trained as educators and have over forty years combined experience in the field on the elementary, secondary, undergraduate, and graduate levels. In our years of experience as classroom teachers, K-12 administrators, college professors and university administrators, we have become experts in how people learn, and how to create and organize structures to help them internalize and apply important concepts. In our opinion, one of the most powerful things about our life together are the lessons we have taken away from our failed marriage experiences, our expertise as master teachers, and the experience of building a successful marriage. This triad poises us in a unique position to share best practices that have been tested and tried through our own experiences in this journey called marriage.

The tools in this book will challenge you by requiring dedication, effort, and 200% of your time (100% from each of you). We know and believe that if you apply yourself with integrity and humility, you will see your personal agendas digress and your marriage progress. Please understand that whenever deep-rooted issues are tampered with and are in jeopardy of being exposed and eradicated, you will probably feel as if you are losing control and becoming an emotional wreck. At times you will be angry, hurt, embarrassed and may lash out at your spouse. Somedays you may be downright annoyed and want to give up. When that occurs, you should give yourself a day or two to breathe and reset from the fatigue of this demanding *heart* work. But, as soon as you have dealt with your emotions and feelings, set up your schedule, and get back to work.

As educators, we have learned that evaluating and modifying is one of the best ways to gain real time feedback, build momentum, and grow in any situation. With this in mind, we created a series of activities designed to walk readers through the application of the content we share throughout the book. As you readers engage in these activities, you will gain information and immediate feedback to enhance your understanding of each other's needs. You will also discover ways to adjust to the shifts in your relationship over time and discard unwanted or unnecessary baggage that could weigh the marriage down. The activities might be difficult at first. However, after you are able to get a handle on your feelings, and trust that you and your spouse have each other's best interests at heart, you will be able to hear, understand, and meet each other's needs. When implemented properly, the tools provided throughout the book will serve as shortcuts to pinpoint issues that need to be addressed, and therefore eliminate a lot of wasted time and energy. It's hard work, but we know that, if you work at it, it will work!

Doing the work to truly see yourself as you are and make any needed positive change are extremely difficult things to do. So, you and your spouse must wholeheartedly accept this challenge. Self-Discovery is the process of doing what is necessary to understand and uncover who you truly are as a person. Self-Discovery is the first step towards becoming a better you. We believe that in a healthy marriage both partners must 1) provide for, 2) invest in, and 3) empower (P.I.E.) one another. Thus, you are on a quest to discover the unique formula for your relationship that makes Marriage Simple as P.I.E.

As you read the book, stay engaged because you will bounce back and forth between both of our vantage points as we did the work to save our failing marriage. Our hope is that providing our two views will help you to see things in your marriage from both sides of the fence. The construct of the book is meant to make you examine your own thinking and actions about specific topics, while providing insight and enlightenment of how your spouse may be viewing the same situation. This one-two punch approach doubles your opportunity to grow.

If you want to dial up the quality of your marriage relationship a few notches, read this book with your partner, and commit to doing the work revealed in the principles, advice and experiences shared within these pages. Building the marriage of your dreams is within your reach, in fact, it is simple as P.I.E.

In this the second edition of our book, we have built and integrated into the Baggage Claim experience a workbook that readers can use as a tool in conjunction with the text. Keep in mind, it is not necessary to engage in the workbook to extract value form the book. However, it is recommended, because after all, action speaks louder than words. There is no right or wrong way to engage with Baggage Claim. You can go chapter by chapter, or finish the book and then move on to the workbook. It is suggested, however, that you follow the directions in the workbook because the activities have been designed to activate your multiple intelligences to ensure the principles being introduced are absorbed and activated into your daily lives. We are so excited that you have committed to the Baggage Claim journey and our prayer is that your commitment will only grow as you progress in this journey one word, page, and chapter at a time.

Pre-Assess your Marriage Prior to Chapter 1

To maintain a healthy marriage, you must commit to always *Provide for, Invest* in, and *Empower* one another. Although those ingredients may operate differently in each relationship, they are consistent ingredients in the recipe of a happy and healthy marriage. The "Assess Your Marriage" activity is designed to help you analyze your relationship and evaluate each of its components so you can be more deliberate in creating a game plan to improve your love affair with your husband or wife.

We suggest you complete this copy of the "Assess Your Marriage "tool BEFORE reading this book to pre-assess your own perception of each of the categories addressed in the tool. This tool is meant to be completed separate from your spouse, which means it is based on YOUR interpretation of each category and YOUR perception of the score it deserves. Once you complete the tool on your own, schedule some time with your spouse to compare and contrast each other's assessments. Don't' be alarmed when your perception and your spouse's perceptions are different. More than likely, they will be. This is an opportunity to talk to one another, listen to one another, ask questions, and get a better understanding of each other's thoughts and feelings. Approach this activity as a learner. Don't look now, but the work of building a better marriage has already begun.

Once you finish reading the whole book, you will complete the post version of the "Assess Your Marriage" tool using the same procedure you used to complete the pre-version. However, this time, include in the discussion of your assessment with your spouse a comparison between your pre- and post-version scores. To create a culture of continuous improvement in your marriage, complete and compare another post version of the tool at the three-month, six-month, and twelve-month marks. This will provide you with some data you can use to track how much your thinking has changed and how far your relationship has progressed. Most importantly, make sure you keep the conversation going.

Rate each category on a scale of 1-10 *(10 the greatest 1 the lowest)*. *Provide a brief reason for the score*

Category	Score	Reason
Goals / Drive/ Aspirations *(Is there a sense that there is a common target or mission that you are accomplishing together?)*		
Sex & Intimacy *(How compatible are your sex drives, definitions of intimacy, and priority levels when it comes to sex and intimacy?)*		

Parenting/ Family Values

(Consider whether your similarities and differences around family values and parenting complement each other or clash. Are they effective or damaging?)

Dealing with Conflict

(Consider how you resolve conflict in your marriage. Do you feel you have a good understanding of how and when to address issues in your relationship?)

Career & Money

(How compatible are you in your style of handling money and prioritizing career?)

Household Responsibilities

(Are you happy with your household responsibilities?)

Communication

(Do you feel like you try your best to understand each other's views, feelings, and opinions?)

Faith / Spirituality / Beliefs

(How spiritually compatible are you? Do you assist in each's spiritual growth?)

Friendship with Each Other

(Is your spouse your best friend?)

Managing External Friendships

(Are external relationships prioritized such that they are a help and not a hinderance to your marriage?)

Add the scores for each category to calculate your **Total Score**

Divide the Total
Score by 10 to calculate
the Average Score of
Your Marriage. *(Total
Score /10)*

Claiming your Baggage
-Kim-

"In order to protect the things that were important to me, I hid them in physical bags. Eventually I became the bag that hid my feelings, emotions, and pain."

Chapter One - Claiming your Baggage

Kim's Self-Discovery

Flying state to state, I've experienced some unfortunate issues with airlines regarding baggage. I've had lost bags, damaged bags, and as my children claim at times, far too many bags! Truthfully, as a little girl, I always carried a bag to school. Those bags always had miscellaneous items that I toted around often for no obvious reason, except for the security of making sure that my belongings were safe. I never understood how this was an issue until I cleaned out my mother's closet after she passed away. I found several dozens of bags with jewelry, perfume, coins, old receipts, and checkbooks with notes and scriptures written on every envelope in any available white space she could find. It was then that I made a connection between her and myself. At first, it was cute and a little funny until I realized that the open spaces that I filled weren't just on paper but in my head, on my heart, and in my life. I call them fearful overloads and lingering distractions.

Now let me be frank; I couldn't see this issue right away. To be honest, it took some years and some tears before I could see how innocently clinging to torn pieces of paper, bags, old envelopes, and unneeded items was the way I dealt with deeper issues of fear, abandonment, and rejection. Honestly, I was extremely resistant to the thought of seeing myself as a physical, mental, or spiritual hoarder. Truthfully, I would have never seen a connection if my husband hadn't exposed the obvious issues of my past that were highlighted to him. Those issues were leaking into all of my relationships and causing me to be a difficult partner in our marriage. This revelation crushed my ability to blame him for our problems. After he shared his experiences with me, I was still clueless, but I was unable to pretend any longer that all was well in my home or my heart! Thankfully now, but hurtfully then, this was the challenging beginning that forced me to claim my baggage and address the land mines that I buried during my childhood.

Seriously, most of the crushing concerns that I remember happened so long ago that I thought I'd overcome them. The truth, however, was that they were dormant and lingering like a hidden tag in an expensive clothing store!

This section is titled "self-discovery," but maybe "discovering self" would be a better title, because the discovery isn't made by you alone. Self-discovery is sometimes exposed by your daughters who avoid talking to you because you fail to see any wrong in yourself; or your sons who purposely say all the right things to make you happy so that you stop complaining because they know

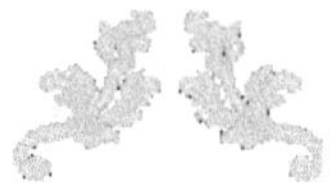

"In order to protect the things that were important to me, I hid them in physical bags. Eventually I became the bag that hid my feelings, emotions and pain."

that you have angle-vision instead of a mirror-view of yourself; or your spouse who retreats into silence to avoid the messy emotional battle that comes from confronting you! Prior to beginning the walk through my journey of discovering self, I still couldn't see what I did that was so wrong or damaging. I packed my belongings in bags so that I didn't lose them or so that no one could find or take my things from me. In order to protect the things that were important to me, I hid them in physical bags. Eventually I became the bag that hid my feelings, emotions, and pain. I wrote messages to myself on paper so that I could log my feelings because no one seemed to care about them. I wrote them down so that I could always go back to remember how I felt or how people hurt me. This was my way to protect myself from getting too close to those who had hurt me in the past. It was the only way I knew to save myself because, as a little girl, I felt that no one else paid attention. It was my way of self-preservation, caring for me, keeping myself from being hurt, judged, abused, attacked, degraded, or ignored.

When I was a little girl, I was neglected and overlooked. I wrote letters to myself so that I could feel important. I paid attention to myself because I felt invisible and thought everyone else was special. Worse, the dysfunction of the household included physical and sexual abuse. There were times that my mother and I were forced to leave our home in the middle of the night with nothing but the clothes we were wearing.

So, I learned to keep my bags packed in case we had to escape again. This way, I wouldn't lose everything again and be at the mercy of a relatives, friends, or strangers. I learned to use harsh words as a wall to keep people at a distance so they could not get close enough to hurt me. To maintain power over my own life, I would point out my own faults before giving anyone else the opportunity to do so. I convinced myself that I didn't need anyone! Thus, I became an expert at suppressing my pain and hiding my wounds. I had suppressed so many of the devastating blows that occurred while growing up that it became easy…It was my norm.

At this point, I could not see the correlation between a few little bags, notes, and suppressing childhood trauma. Honestly, anyone operating in a survival mentality would not have seen the connection either. Today, I know that the plot of the enemy was to sidetrack me so that I felt misplaced and twisted, such that suppressing issues became natural and facing my truth seemed unnatural. So, for years, I suppressed.

Suppressing is like filling a bottle. Eventually it gets so full, and when there is no more room, there will either be an explosion or leakage, and that's what Newt could see. There was so much baggage that I couldn't stuff anything else inside of me, so I was leaking and exploding everywhere. It got so weird and familiar that I couldn't escape it, even if I wanted to! Small reminders like familiar smells and sounds took me to dark places that I thought time had cured. Unfortunately, I began to create assumptions of people. I also overprotected children and relatives because I was paranoid. I guess I was establishing self-fulfilling prophecies, which caused me to block innocent people from my life for no reason at all. It was the only way that I knew how to take care of me, and, until I began the process of discovering self, it worked just fine!

STOP AND PONDER

Claiming your baggage or discovering things about yourself doesn't mean that you have to relive the pain of the past. What it means is that you must admit and face what happened and find a way to work through the lingering effects of those experiences so you can be whole and live outside of the bondage instead of it living inside of you. Take time now to think of those imaginary force fields that you've put up to protect yourself. Get a pencil and some paper and write them down. Today, you have the upper hand and the power to address the lies they have been speaking in your ear and denounce the dominion that you have given them over your life. These are your bags—no one else's. You're the only one who can use them to change the paralyzing effect they have had in your past and use them to propel you into your future.

Hopefully, I've shared something that helps you to walk directly into your own mine field; and as you walk, each step will cause an explosion of the baggage that you have hidden and suppressed. I pray that the mess it leaves forces you to see what's been hiding in plain view so that you begin the clean-up process. So, hold on tight and fasten your seatbelt because there's so much more to come.

2
───────────

Claiming your Baggage
Newt

"As I began to address the baggage in my life, I started to see patterns and similarities in the bags that I had accumulated throughout my life. In essence, I kept having the same issues over and over - so much so, that they became part of me. And here's the kicker, I never realized that they were issues."

Chapter Two - Claiming Your Baggage

Newt's Self-Discovery

Looking back over my life, I was a chameleon. There were several roles I played depending upon the environment in which I placed myself and what I needed to adapt to survive. I remember being the young athlete where my only concern and ambition was to make it to the party on the weekend and impress as many girls as possible. I phased into the young college student who was open to new people and new things. Full of dreams and aspirations, I never slowed down long enough to effectively plot a path to accomplish any of them. Because, like many other young people in their early 20s, I knew everything and didn't need anyone's advice. As I grew into a young man, the goals that I failed to accomplish because of my choices began to erode my self-image. The self-destructive behaviors that were once considered fun and innocent began forming habits that acted as weights and hindrances standing in the way of the type of forward progress I knew I was capable of. As I crossed into my late 30s and early 40s, my mind was going a mile a minute. I was stuck in the mud, spinning wheels, and not moving forward at all. Many people would look at me externally and think I was accomplished. After all, I had a wonderful wife and seven awesome children, five of which we had the privilege of raising in our household. We owned a home, drove nice cars, had professional degrees, and enjoyed great careers. From the outside in, what more could anyone from my humble beginnings ask?

When I hit my mid-40s, I was able to look back and understand that those phases in my life were roles I played because I had never taken the time to be introduced to me. As it turns out, it was a pleasure to meet me, and become acquainted with the greatness and potential I possessed. When I became acquainted with the true me, it was a free-ing and unbinding experience. I no longer had to put on a façade or play a role to be what I thought people expected of me. I could simply be myself. There was only one problem - although I was introduced to myself, there was still a long process of self-discovery that I had to endure to actually know myself.

As I moved from phase to phase throughout my lifetime playing whatever role was necessary for me to survive, I began to collect baggage that became a part of me. The thing is, collecting the baggage and adopting it as a part of my life was not something I was doing consciously. It was a natural grafting that occurred as a result of the path I was walking, the character I was adopting, and the things (good and bad) I chose to do.

If it was up to me, I would have ignored the whole "self-discovery" process. However, if I was going to have a happy and productive marriage, be a good example for my sons and daughters, and quite frankly, maintain the respect of my family, I had to turn and face the baggage that I had accumulated throughout the years. It was apparent that, when I looked inside that baggage ,I was going to discover the what and why behind my current actions and decisions. I was going to discover why I was unable to let go of the weights and hindrances that were in the way of my becoming that awesome version of me that somehow could never surface. I am still unable to explain it, but I was terrified to claim that baggage.

Let me make it very clear; this need for self-discovery is not some-thing I invented. I didn't wake up one day and say hey, let's discover "you" so that you can be a better "you." Nope, as much as I'd like to take credit for it, my wife was very instrumental. She kept a strategic and continuous amount of pressure on me until I realized that there were things I needed to address. Periodically, she would say little things to me like, "You just don't have any rules in your life, do you?", or, "One day God's going to pull the sheet off your mess. You should take care of it before He does." After she said her piece, she would go back to loving and supporting me, and doing all the things that she had done throughout the years to continue to make our house a home.

I was nursing an addiction and hiding poor choices of my past. As a result, I had developed two opposite sides to my life. One side was my "on the stage" persona. He was super positive and very helpful to those in need, especially the students and staff in the schools he led. The other side was simply a mess. He disappeared for days at a time, wasted much needed household funds, put poison in his physical body, expected his wife to carry both his responsibility and hers, and put his wife in a position of hiding his issues to protect him and the children from being affected.

As I began to address the baggage in my life, I started to see patterns and similarities in the bags that I had accumulated throughout my life. In essence, I kept having the same issues over and over - so much so, that they became part of me, and here's the kicker, I never realized that they were issues.

As Kim warned, the sheets were pulled back and my secret was exposed; and to put it mildly, the whole family was disrupted. I had to make a crucial decision. Either I was going to give in and fall all the way down the tubes or submit to the uphill journey of recovery to normalcy. I chose to begin to submit to the journey of self-discovery and face the bags I had accumulated over the years. I recall it being a very painful and lonely process. Years of embarrassing and shameful memories were front and center. I had to face my broken character and the poor judgement I had exercised. It was a somber and sobering experience. I was feeling unfulfilled because it became apparent that, for many years, I had been just chasing my tail. I was caught in a loop that I couldn't even see. As I began to address the baggage in my life, I started to see patterns and similarities in the bags that I had accumulated through-out my life. In essence, I kept having the same issues over and over -

so much so, that they became part of me. Here's the kicker, I never realized they were issues.

Self-discovery requires that you claim your baggage. For me, claiming my baggage meant two things.

1. I had to recognize and own the fact that choices, experiences, and things that I was subjected to throughout my life became the things I held on to and carried with me everywhere I went. In essence, I discovered that my baggage was keeping me from becoming me, because somehow, I came to the conclusion that it was what defined me. Claiming my baggage meant that I had to own and admit that I was unable to progress in my life because of that baggage I had unconsciously accumulated but refused to let go.

2. Claiming my baggage meant that all I had to do was just that—*claim it*. In other words, I did not have to carry it with me; I just needed to acknowledge that it was mine. In fact, once I could claim the baggage, it made it much easier for me to put it down and do the work to walk away from it.

Don't get it twisted - distancing yourself from your baggage is no easy task. My early days of consciously doing that work were some of the most difficult days in my life. If you want to discover yourself so you can live more fulfilled and productive; if you want to finally exhale and be fine with yourself, just as you are, then dealing with what you unpack from your baggage is necessary and unavoidable. Keep in mind that self-discovery is a lifelong journey and one that is best traveled hand-in-hand with your spouse. Remember, it was Kim who urged me to face my issues. Your spouse won't always understand what you're feeling and how the things that are revealed as you claim your baggage are affecting you. In most cases, they will understand that the journey is necessary, and their support will make it easier for you to travel. So, if you keep in mind that the work required to deal with what surfaces is *your* work to do, your spouse will appreciate and admire your transparency, and stand by your side as you address those things. I don't know how they do it, but they have a way of magically changing something you have avoided for years—something that caused you pain and discomfort—into the very thing that you crave to do.

Chapter 1 & 2 Reflect Upon This

What are bags? Bags are Personality Traits or Character Issues you take with you wherever you go. They show up and have an effect on every one of your personal and professional relationships and interactions with others.

What personality traits may be impacting your personal and professional relationships?

Chapter 1 & 2 Workbook Activity

It is suggested that you complete Activity #2 in the Baggage Claim Workbook, can significantly enhance your understanding of both yourself and your spouse, fostering deeper connections and communication. This activity prompts you to identify strengths and weaknesses in your personalities, enabling a profound exploration of your individual traits and those of your partner.

Embracing this exercise empowers you to recognize not only your own qualities but also those of your significant other. This leads to greater empathy, understanding, and appreciation. By delving into this activity, you'll pave the way for improved communication, stronger bonds, and a more harmonious relationship built on mutual comprehension and acceptance. Embrace this opportunity to discover and celebrate the unique traits that make both you and your spouse special.

3

———————

Beneath the Surface - Kim

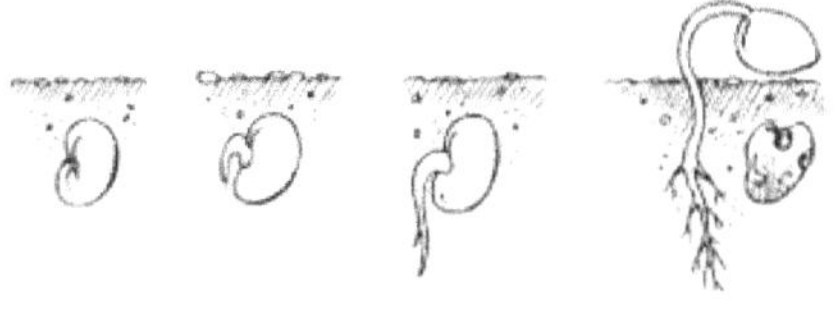

*"Sadly, his feelings
towards me, were like
seeds which produced a
harvest of negative
thoughts and feelings that
I embraced about myself."*

Chapter Three - Beneath the Surface

KIM - ABANDONED & ABUSED

The mirror became my best unresponsive friend. Often, I'd look in the mirror and ask myself, "What's going on with you? Why are you battling inside with yourself and everyone else?" and "What does all this mean?" Many times, I thought about how young my mother was when she had me and if she was devastated that her life completely changed as a result of my birth. I believe that she was only 16 when she got pregnant and about 17 when I was born. I can't even imagine not being able to enjoy my teenage years, dances, dating, hanging with friends, traveling, and high school life! To me, being young and free was the best time of my life. After thinking about it, I realize that she was just a kid who was looking for the attention she needed. She found it in a cute boy who was willing to share some of his time with her. Honestly, my dad was just as young as my mom, and neither of them were ready to commit to a relationship and act as adults who have a child. No wonder it was a challenge for me because it was extremely difficult for them.

Growing up, I remember close relationships with my aunts, uncles, and grandparents. Thank God for family! But I don't remember having a close relationship with either of my parents. Don't get me wrong, I believe and know that they were both too young to give a little girl the attention she needed, so the "village" chipped in and raised me. I remember living with my grandparents for a while, but so much of that is a blur because I was so young. I do remember the love they showed me, and they are memories I still hold dear! Not long after that, my mother got married, and suddenly moved **me** from the home of Nanny Ruth (my mother's mom) to live with her and her new husband in a big new home with three inherited siblings I didn't know at the time. Unfortunately, it was a recipe for disaster, but no one knew at that time what we were headed toward, especially me!

Life with my new family was completely different than what I was used to, and I could tell immediately that my mother's husband wasn't happy about my presence. He made that obvious every time he looked my way. I was in the way, well, at least in his way. He didn't hesitate to let me know that I didn't fit into the plans that he had for my mother and his children. I remember one day my mother and I ran out of the house. She threw me in the back of her car and yelled, "Kim, lay down on the floor!" I remember looking out the rear window watching my stepfather standing in the middle of the street with his gun shooting toward the back of my mom's car as she sped away. With that horrible memory, all I knew was that he wanted my mom and me dead, and he wasn't afraid to do it in front of the entire neighborhood.

Sadly, his feelings towards me, were like seeds which produced a harvest of negative thoughts and feelings that I embraced about myself.

After spending a few days at Nanny Ruth's house, my mom took me to my father's parents' house. This house was a place of safety and love, and I was happy to be there! I remember crying and begging my father's mother, who I affectionately called "Na-na" not to let my mom take me back, because "that man doesn't like me." After listening to my story, when my mother came to pick me up, my grandparents talked her into letting me live with them. At that time, my dad was in the Army, so he wasn't around; but that was okay with me because my dad's family was the best. I knew that I was finally safe. Well, at least for two weeks until Nanny Ruth found out that my mom had left me to live with grandma Na-Na. Nanny Ruth felt that she had given me away and forced my mom come and get me and take me back to that house of my fears with her husband.

I know that if Nanny Ruth knew how bad things were at my mom's house, she wouldn't have made me go back there. I wasn't allowed to tell her anything; that was how it worked in our family: "What's happens here stays here!" After I got older, I realized that my mom was trying to keep me safe, and that was the reason she took me to my father's parents. She knew that they loved me, and they would never judge her for her choices.

Truthfully, my mother was petrified of her husband; but it still wasn't enough for her to stay away from him. I never understood my mother's reason for going back to him, especially after he shot at us. The worst part was that she took me back there knowing that he didn't like me and made it very clear that he couldn't stand my birth father. As a little girl, I couldn't understand what I did to make him hate me. Sadly, his feelings towards me were like seeds which produced a harvest of negative thoughts and feelings that I embraced about myself. I didn't believe anyone should or could love me; I didn't even love myself! Life was difficult! I felt like an ugly, horribly bad, unwanted child for whom no one cared. I hated myself and became angrier with the world when he beat me or called me names and intimidated me with his glares. Since I knew my mom was afraid of him, I didn't tell her anything that was happening to me. She, out of fear, used threats to keep me quiet around her siblings, who would have instantly intervened. Perhaps she was afraid of my stepfather harming them. Throughout my young adult years, even when my mother and he separated, I battled with self-hate and low self-esteem. The seed had been planted.

At that time, I couldn't comprehend why my mother didn't protect me. The truth is, because it was normal, I grew to believe that I deserved the treatment. Every day was a challenge. I walked on egg-shells and stood in corners for years. Today, I can understand my mother's reasons for tolerating his behavior to survive. Sadly, the need for survival will make you do things you would never dream of doing. My mother had grown up feeling rejected, and since I wasn't born with instructions, she could only do what she knew. So, she raised me to live in a world where I felt that no one cared about me and no one could save me!

But God gave me an ally: my stepsister. Finally, someone cared about me and loved me. Although she was only four years older than me, she tried her best to shield me from the torture and mistreatment she witnessed! Honestly, she acted more like a mother to me than my own mother. At that point in my life, I was afraid of everything so, I would cling on to her arm and close my eyes while I walked so that I couldn't see anything frightening. My sister did what my mom couldn't do. She defended me and stood-up to her own father. My sister was the apple of his eye, and he would do anything she told him to do! She used her power over him to protect me.

Unfortunately, there were times when she wasn't around, and at those times, I became the victim of another relative's sexual assaults. One day, this relative was caught in the act of assaulting me. However, instead of being protected or cared for, my mother's husband beat me until I was unconscious. When I came to, I was in the dark in the basement of his house. Again, my mother's fear of her husband caused her to press me with threats to keep the molestation a secret. That day was the last time I spoke of the abuse until I told my husband, Newt, almost 40 years later. In retrospect, as I reflect on what the major drivers were beneath the surface that caused me to act and think as I did, they would be fear and pain. I never wanted anyone to feel or experience the abandonment and abuse I had to endure. So, I learned to sacrifice myself to protect everyone else.

4

Beneath the Surface
- Newt -

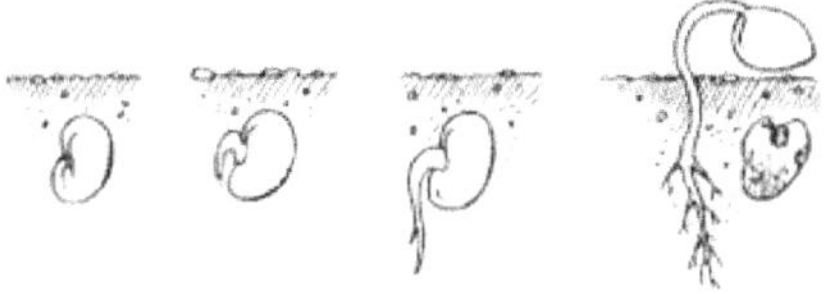

"That stigma influenced me in ways that no one could have predicted. My self-esteem was depleted as I began to accept that I couldn't meet the expectations that the culture of my household and upbringing dictated."

Chapter Four - Beneath the Surface

Newt - Self-Worth and Self-Esteem

If you owned a small business and hired an accountant, the first thing he or she would do is ask for all your financial records concerning the business from the first day the business started. The accountant would reconcile your accounts and determine exactly how much money you have. When you enter the union of marriage the same principle must be applied. You must reflect upon the things that have influenced you throughout your life so you can better determine the things that have shaped you into the individual you are today. As you partner with your spouse, it is important that you truly understand what's beneath the surface making you tick.

As I reflect on my childhood and many other things that shaped my thoughts, attitudes, and character as I grew into an adult, I have both fond, and not-so-fond memories. I grew up in a two-parent working-class household with two older sisters. My father was 40 years old when I was born, and my mother was 30; boy, did they have their hands full. Both my parents were born in the Jim Crow-ruled south, where there were few opportunities for Black folks. They moved to the northeastern part of the United States to create a better life for themselves and their children. As a result, there was a culture in our household which dictated that you push yourself and strive to always be the best. It didn't matter whether it was in sports, school, or how you were viewed by the other adults in the community; we were expected always to excel and favorably represent our family name.

There's absolutely nothing wrong with those expectations, and I am truly grateful to my parents for creating an atmosphere of accountability and excellence. The things they taught me and the personal drive I've developed as a result of my upbringing have ultimately helped me to live a productive and happy life. I understand that my parents wanted me to be great and did what they knew to create a culture that would cultivate the mindset in me to meet those expectations. However, not all human beings are the same, and we must allow some variability for them to adjust and respond in ways that align with their individuality. In my generation, that was not a popular approach. The weight of those expectations without accepting the mistakes that I would make along the way had a major impact on my development. Therefore, I had tremendous difficulty in developing positive self-esteem and finding value in my self-worth.

Let me explain. I was a skinny, buck-toothed boy with average athletic ability and pretty good intellectual dexterity in the classroom. I watched my father go back to school and get his advanced degrees. Each degree he obtained yielded an almost immediate change in his professional pursuits, which resulted in consistent increases in our quality of living. My mother was a hard worker with a stellar reputation among both adults and children throughout the community. She was known for helping anyone who needed assistance. My sisters—eight years and six years older than me, respectively—were high achievers. For example, my oldest sister graduated from high school a year early. Thus, in my mind, I had a two tough acts to follow.

Finding my way as a young boy was tough, and I carried a heavy weight. I believed that I if I was not the best, I was a failure. I developed an all or nothing attitude - when I was good, I was good, but when I wasn't, I was really bad. I didn't know how to give myself a break and allow myself permission to make a mistake. I did not relate well with adults and authority figures, so, I was constantly in trouble at school. I had a hard time fitting into structured events and organized sports. As a result, I conflicted with my peers and got into many verbal and physical altercations.

My behaviors became the focus of conversation and attention that I was given by my parents and other adult authority

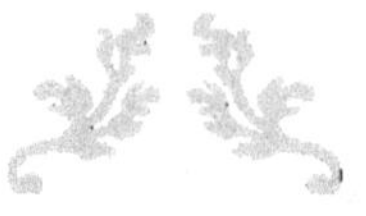

> **That stigma influenced me in ways that no one could have predicted. My self-esteem was depleted as I began to accept that I couldn't meet the expectations that the culture of my household and upbringing dictated.**

figures in my life. Thus, they became a major focus for me. As a result, I began to conclude that I was a "bad" kid. In fact, around the neighborhood, all the adults called me "bad little Newt." That stigma influenced me in ways no one could have predicted. My self-esteem was depleted as I began to accept that I couldn't meet the expectations dictated by the culture of my household and my upbringing. I felt I was worthless and had no value, so I was content with the attention I got for negative behaviors because it provided a false sense of worth or value. At least when I was in trouble, the spotlight and focus were on me.

As I began to grow and mature into a man, I compensated for my deficiencies in self-esteem and self-worth by self-medicating. Juggling a full-blown addiction and a desire to walk in my positive purpose, I created two divisions in my life. In one division, I was able to create a very positive and impactful professional life that was respected and helpful to many. The other division was dark and undisciplined, driven by addiction, and lacking rules and accountability. As time went on, these two divisions of my life began to grow and move dangerously close to each other. My positive side became more positive and gained great respect from others outwardly, and my dark side grew darker and less accountable to rules. As a result, I felt hypocritical and lived with a great deal of guilt.

When I met my wife, she was attracted to my positive side. But it wasn't long before the darker side of me began to surface in my choices, conduct, and attitude. Of course, I had no idea that I was as far gone as I was, nor did I understand where the struggle originated or why I had to wrestle it. After years of steady decline, the two divisions of my life collided, I was exposed, and an explosion occurred in my life. Someone once said that renovation often requires demolition. In hindsight, I believe that this explosion was my chance to renovate my life. The problem was that I had no idea how to do so because I didn't know what served as the foundation that influenced me to live my life the way I was.

I had to do what the accountant taking on a new client would do. I had to take a detailed look at all of the contributions and patterns of influence in my life as far back as I could remember. It was then that I realized that the pressure meant to motivate me to excel and be productive did that, and more. As a result of the expectations my family instilled, I developed the work ethic and the diligence to be productive. However, I was also very hard on myself when I made a mistake or fell short of the target. I didn't understand that failing is part of the growth process. It's a normal thing that all people experience. Instead, I became unforgiving, self-judgmental, and began to question my value and worth. This resulted in compromised esteem issues which put a strain on any existing and future relationships I would develop.

I know this is a book about marriage, but you must understand if you want to have a healthy union, you have to do a deep dive into the things that impacted and influenced your development into the person that you are today. That is the person you are bringing into the marriage. That is the person your spouse will have to live with day in and day out. In my case, my parents instilled a healthy sense of high expectations intending to help me be productive. However, they triggered a self-devaluing cycle that led to poor decisions, guilt, low self-esteem, and difficulty in maintaining relationships.

Doing the work to reflect upon root causes that impacted your development can be difficult and painful work, but it's worth it. The benefits that you will reap in your ability to relate with your spouse because you have a better understanding of yourself are greater than you can imagine. When you are in touch with what has historically framed your reactions and responses, then you are more in control of the responses and reactions you make in the future. This will directly enhance the quality of the relationship with your spouse. So, are you willing to do the work?

Warning! This may be the most difficult exercise you have attempted. When you start digging into your own psyche, you may find things there that are difficult to face. You may see and feel emotions that make you feel sick inside. This is your inoculation! Press forward. Submit to the process, and don't quit on yourself. Facing that dark place shines a light on it. But just before the light breaks through, you will encounter feelings of embarrassment, shame, difficulty admitting the faults of your parents, or the pain of reliving the actions of your abuser. You may discover things about yourself that you don't like. And you may discover things about people you love that are equally hard to face. We know from experience because we have both been there. This is not easy. But it's necessary. More importantly, it is rewarding. Yes, you will have to brave the dark caverns of your memories, pain, and emotions. But you will emerge renewed, empowered, and strengthened. You will emerge feeling cleansed and reborn.

Chapter 3 & 4 Reflect Upon This

Many of us have spent the majority of our lives dealing with positive and negative comments about ourselves. For the most part, we seem to do okay with the comments, at least until we have to look in the mirror and address the issues ourselves.

As a result of the personality traits you identified when reflecting upon chapter two, what behaviors are your common behaviors, and how might they be limiting your relationships?

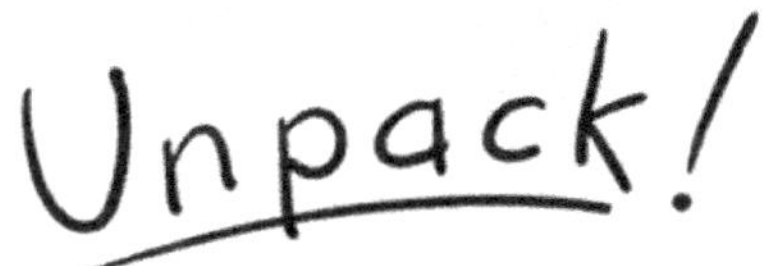

Chapter 3 & 4 Workbook Activity

Chapters 3 & 4 align with Activity #3 in the Baggage Claim Workbook. Participating in this activity holds immense value as it builds upon the foundation laid in Activity #2. By mapping behaviors and tendencies stemming from the personality traits identified in Activity #2, you delve deeper into understanding the intricate connections between traits and actions.

This activity serves as a guiding compass, allowing you to recognize patterns and associations between your personalities and your behaviors or reactions. Embracing Activity #3 lays the foundation of the roadmap for navigating potential conflicts or misunderstandings. Engaging in this activity will undoubtedly pave the way for a more nuanced understanding of yourselves, fostering a deeper and more harmonious relationship built on mutual insight and comprehension. Dive into this exploration with an open mind, and you'll discover valuable insights that can enrich and strengthen your bond.

Uncovered - Kim

"I wasn't aware that these unresolved issues were the weights that could eventually sink all of my relationships."

Chapter Five - Uncovered

Kim's Intense Protection

About one year after the basement incident, my stepfather's anger issues spilled out of our home and into the community. After a heated confrontation, he took a man's life and spent several years in prison for murder. Because of his absence while incarcerated, I finally had my mom back. She was free and, apparently, intended to enjoy that freedom even though she had three kids depending on her. Every weekend without fail, mom was out on the town. My aunt was old enough to take care of my little brother, sister, and me so most weekends she helped watch us. By this time, I had a field of secrets, hills of resentment, mountains of pain, and an ocean of mistrust. I was a little woman at the age of seven! I was mean, hateful, and hurtful; and it didn't matter who I poured it on. Everyone deserved it because no one saved me, and that was the way it was going to be!

Finally, my birth father came home from the military, but he had his own family - him, his wife, and their daughter. My little sister and I had visits with him every weekend and all summer. My dad was so sweet and kind to me. However, I was mad at him as well, and he didn't even know it. All I could think of was that he wasn't here to protect me because he was taking care of his new family. I was also terribly upset that I had to share my dad with his new family—his wife and stepdaughter. I wanted him to myself, and, truthfully, I needed him! I thought, here we go again. I have to be with people I don't know, and the last time that happened, I suffered many forms of abuse. Out of fear, I was very protective of my baby sister to make sure no one hurt her! I vowed to keep her safe because no one kept me safe. Again, I didn't tell anyone how I felt because the last time someone knew my pain, I was beaten and put in a dark basement! So, as the vicious cycle dictated, I suppressed everything again!

I wasn't aware that these unresolved issues were the weights that could eventually sink all of my relationships.

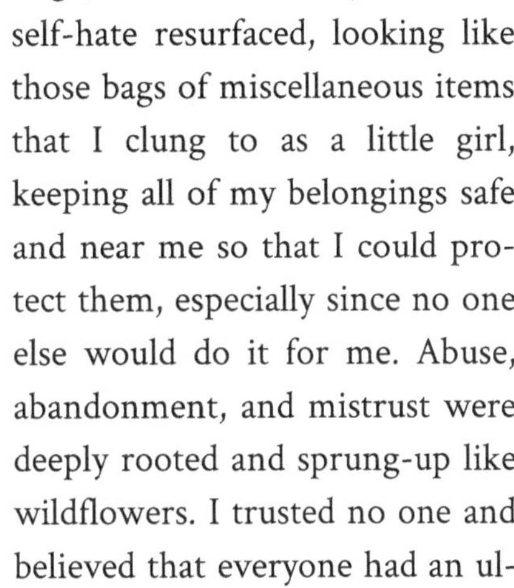

Unfortunately, in my first marriage, that childhood rejection and self-hate resurfaced, looking like those bags of miscellaneous items that I clung to as a little girl, keeping all of my belongings safe and near me so that I could protect them, especially since no one else would do it for me. Abuse, abandonment, and mistrust were deeply rooted and sprung-up like wildflowers. I trusted no one and believed that everyone had an ulterior motive. The fear of being taken advantage of manifested a focused and intense argumentative behavior that took a "fight or flight stance." Keep in mind that when you're used to being in your own skin, you can't look from the outside of a situation, and you don't see what others can see in you. As I said before, it wasn't until I finally listened to what Newt was saying that I could see the damage and difficulties I was presenting in my marriage. It was then that I was able to claim my baggage and begin my own healing which saved my second marriage.

Sad to say, at this point, my bags were full. As I continued to look deeper into my issues, there was so much I needed to address. I wasn't aware that these unresolved issues were the weights that could eventually sink all of my relationships. In addition to the pain, there was doubt, mistrust, suspicion, and low-self-worth; these feelings were bottled up inside of me for years. I didn't know the same forces that charged my emotions and feelings as a child were also driving my behaviors as an adult. These issues appeared to be time-released showing up little by little in each area of my life.

Just a few months after my first marriage was over, I met this wonderful person, Newt, who appeared to be everything I wanted, and we were getting closer every day. When we met, I told Newt what I wanted him to know about me. You know how we do… when we first meet someone, we only show them the best parts of ourselves, thinking that we can erase the parts we hate. I convinced myself to believe that the only reason I was an insecure, guarded, angry person in my previous marriage was that my first husband wasn't what God wanted for me. I blamed our problems on his immaturity and lack of respect for me. We were unequally yoked, I said. These are the usual justifications or churchy sayings that we fool ourselves into believing when we refuse to accept responsibility for our contribution to our failing situations in life.

As humiliating as it is to say, I believed all of that nonsense, blaming all of my behaviors and actions on everyone else. The worst thing about my presentation to Newt was that I believed it, and so did he. How does that happen? Well, it's easy; it happens when we allow feelings and emotions to determine our choices! We become blind and deaf to reality. It's in this state that we choose to believe the fantasy, only because it sounds and feels better. Blind and in love is how my second relationship began. Neither of us knew that we weren't ready, and we had no idea of all the work that was ahead of us. However, considering the way we felt about each other at that time, I'm not sure if it would have changed our decision to be together. So, we jumped into the marriage headfirst. Early on, Newt could see that I was a beautifully independent, responsible mother who loved her children. I also loved his children, evidenced by the way I cared for them. But he had no idea what was underneath the surface as a result of the years of suppressing my own pain from the horrifying episodes I experienced as a child. I had this pent-up need to control my surroundings in order to keep everything and everyone safe and protected. At any cost, I was prepared to do whatever it took to block any unnecessary pain or danger from invading the space that was familiar to me and those I loved. This umbrella of over-protection appeared as a deep and intense need to control and manage everything, which would have an adverse impact on all of the things I would bring to the table, and unknowingly the people I was trying to protect. In my journey to discover self, dark episodes from my past were exposed, which caused me to stumble upon the key to unlocking the reasons behind my intense need to protect... I was finally uncovered.

6

Uncovered - Newt

"I was faced with the task
of choosing who and what
I was going to be from
that point forward, not for
anyone else, but for me.."

Chapter Six - Uncovered

Newt's Game of Hide and Go Seek

One thing every human being craves is significance. We all seek a sense of belonging. Sometimes we look for that in organizations, individuals, and sometimes in arenas that are not even directly connected to us at all. Significance and belonging are very influential, and, if not consciously checked, can drive us to make choices that lead to self-destructive actions. Although seeking significance is a very real and common cycle that exists in the lives of many, it often goes undetected and unrealized until a drastic mistake or tragic event occurs.

One of the things I found myself doing in my quest for significance and belonging was hiding who I was at that moment. Let me explain. Although I believe that we are all created with a purpose–on purpose— we often make choices that cause us to stray away from that purpose. When this occurs, we appear to be a different individual than we really are. What I mean by that is, there is a seed of purpose embedded within the very fabric of our being. That seed fuels the internal drive to accomplish that purpose. As long as we're moving toward that accomplishment, we feel fulfilled and driven. When we make choices that cause us to stray away from that purpose, even though we're still moving forward, we feel unfulfilled, and a sense of urgency hangs over us. That sense of unfulfillment and urgency can cause anxiety that we often try to subdue by replacing it with some type of approval from others.

Sounds simple, right? If this is the case, then all we have to do is start making choices that cultivate that internal seed which defines our purpose or what we were intended to accomplish. That is correct - the solution is simple, but the solution is also the problem. What you were exposed to, who was speaking in your ear as an impressionable young person, and what your social environment told you that you were capable of accomplishing, all contributed to shaping your thoughts and beliefs about yourself. Those variables were in the environments where you were raised even before you were born. Thus, they became what defined our expectations and created the standard operating procedures that defined our culture or our way of life. In other words, natural events about which we didn't even think twice were the factors that have shaped our thoughts and beliefs about ourselves. The effect that they were having on us was undetectable. So, there was no reason to be alarmed or alerted to any negative or hindering effects that they might have. Here's the kicker, the greatest effect that those factors had on many of us was to prevent us from fully seeing our own purpose, and more importantly, our ability to accomplish it. That is a huge destiny changer!

Let me get back to the point. I grew up in a household where my mother and my father encouraged conversations about our vision, our future, and what we want to ultimately accomplish in life. So, I had some inkling of my purpose, my direction, what I could do to be productive and make an impact in this world as early as my middle school years. Thus, when I started making choices that were counterproductive to following through with the things that I needed to do to walk towards my dreams, goals, and aspirations, quite frankly, I was ashamed of myself. I mean, after all, I knew better. I wasn't raised that way; and there was no reason for me to cut school, lie, steal, self-medicate or any of the other negative things I was doing other than I was seeking significance and wanting to belong. My problem was that I was choosing to belong to the wrong group.

Despite my issues, I did not stop pursuing my dreams, goals, and aspirations. I got a scholarship to go to college to be a civil engineer, which was what I had always dreamed of becoming. As long as I was at the small Historically Black College University (HBCU), Lincoln University of Pennsylvania to which I received my scholarship, I did very well. Actually, I was an outstanding student. It was a sheltered environment with like-minded people who were all exhibiting a certain set of values, morals, and drive targeted towards accomplishing goals and creating a better self. As long as I was there, I belonged to a positive group, and my significance was satisfied because I did well academically and socially in that group. But I transferred to a larger, mainstream, Predominately White Institution (PWI), the Pennsylvania State University, better known as Penn State main campus, and all restrictions were removed. Due to my lack of maturity, I was unable to manage myself and establish the discipline to focus on my studies. Somehow, I forgot the reason I was there in the first place. I wasn't doing any work, so following the principle of reciprocity, I reaped what I sowed and received failing grades!

In hindsight, maybe I should have pushed the pause button and gone back to that positive network that I was a part of in previous years, been transparent, and asked for help. Instead, I decided to hide from them and go elsewhere to seek the significance and belonging for which I longed. Hiding from that network is a very significant part of the story. The hiding is what drove my seeking. The more I sought for things in the wrong places, the more severe my compromising actions became, thus the more I felt that I had to hide, which, of course, drove me to another place to seek significance and belonging; and the cycle continued. No, actually it wasn't a cycle; it was a downward spiral! Throughout the years, I found my life spiraling back around to familiar positive places. The problem was, each time I saw something familiar and positive, I was carrying a heavier load of memories of compromising actions. As a result, the shame and guilt associated with those memories blocked any thought of approaching opportunities to get help from that network. The guilt and shame of those memories triggered the need to make a fight or flight decision, and for many years I chose flight (hiding). That hiding resulted in my inability to simply reach out and grab a lifeline whenever one of those familiar positive places or people were in my path. In hindsight, I'm sure they would have been more than willing to help me up out of the holes into which I had gotten myself.

As you can imagine, I wasn't just having problems managing my own choices and actions; I was having problems deciding exactly what I felt, believed, and thought about myself. Every time I played hide and seek with my life, I was compromising my own self-esteem and self-image. So, I'm sure you can imagine that maintaining a relationship with another human being was tremendously difficult, at best. My mother, father, and sisters represented positivity and "the right thing," but I associated them to my own failure. Thus, they reminded me of the guilt and shame I was carrying. I ostracized myself from them. Hiding from them enabled me to justify my actions and create excuses that allowed me to transfer the responsibility for my own well-being onto someone else.

I literally killed my first marriage. We were both young, idealistic, and full of fairy tale and fantasy-like ideas that were tremendously unrealistic. What we thought we were getting into wasn't what we were getting into at all. Given all of that, even if I wasn't playing hide and go seek, I'm not sure if that relationship would've lasted. But I do believe that my game of hide and go seek is what brought it to a screeching halt much sooner.

Years later, I found myself in love with another beautiful young lady: Kim. She was very responsible, independent, had her own job, apartment, was raising her three kids by herself. She was well-known in the community, and tremendously talented. Most importantly, I was looking at her, and she was looking at me. I was in heaven! What more could I ask? Her care and attention for all the children, both hers and mine, as well as her care of me satisfied the sense of belonging I was seeking. Her good name and accomplishments in the community satisfied the sense of significance I was craving.

Additionally, she was someone to love. She appreciated everything I did for her and made a big deal over it. Again, my need for significance and belonging were satisfied. My whole world stopped. I loved that feeling; it had been what I was seeking since I was a young child. At that time, all I could think of was how I could seal the deal and be with this woman for the rest of my life.

Well, it wasn't long before reality reminded me that I was playing hide-and-go-seek. I had finally found someone who was safe, positive, and possessed everything that I needed to help me to be productive, accomplished and fulfilled from that point forward in my life. So, the seek part was taken care of. But the hiding part raised its ugly head and forced me to have to face myself.

Although Kim was exactly what I needed in my life to fill the gaps and satisfy my yearning to belong, and have significance in a place that mattered, the guilt in the shame of my past that I was hiding drove me to once again go back into hiding. Like any good hide-and-go-seek player, deception, and dishonesty were called on to throw Kim off my true scent. I figured if I could somehow illuminate the good, useful, and commendable parts of me, they would overshadow and minimize the dark side of poor decisions, setbacks, habits, and character choices that made up the baggage that I was bringing with me into the relationship. To make a long story short, Kim's a smart girl and quickly saw through to the real me. I guess it was obvious when I didn't show up to pick her up from work one day because I chose to listen to addiction instead of love, covenant, and responsibility.

However, what she saw wasn't exactly what I saw in myself and predicted that everyone else saw when they looked at me. Of course, she saw my issues, or at least what I wasn't doing such a great job of hiding, but she also saw more positivity and value in me than I had ever seen in myself. So, guess what - she stayed and chose to love me just how I was.

You would think that should be enough for a person to get Honest, Open, and Willing (HOW) with their partner and submit to input so they can begin to do the work to make changes in their life. But not me... No way... Not me! I had gotten too good at and comfortable with hiding. Hiding had driven every choice I had made in my life since I was in middle school when I first put a foreign substance in my body. Quite frankly, I was afraid to stop hiding. To myself, I was a monster. I was there with me for every poor decision and compromised action in which I chose to take part. I knew the whole story from beginning to end. I understood that I had no reason to do the things that I had done, and that I was squarely at the center of fault and responsibility for those choices. I was afraid to admit that truth because I thought that it would make me appear to be a jacked up and confused individual to everyone else, just as I had grown to think of myself. Fast forward 12 years, Kim (for some reason I still can't explain today) was still by my side. I knew she was truly a virtuous woman. But again, the law of reciprocity decided to cash in, and my compromised character choices collided with the positive, productive choices I was making resulting in an explosive catastrophe of exposure. Suddenly I was caught, and everyone knew my secret. There was no more hiding, and it seemed as if what I had been seeking for all my life (significance and belonging), would now never be attained. I was faced with the task of choosing who and what I was going to be from that point forward, not for anyone else, but for me. For the first time in my life, I realized that I mattered and what I thought of me was up to me. To make a long story short, I sought after and submitted to the help that I needed to address the addiction and begin a long healing and recovery process. That process helped me become aware of many things. The most important was, in order to get what I was seeking (significance and belonging), the first thing I had to do was to stop hiding.

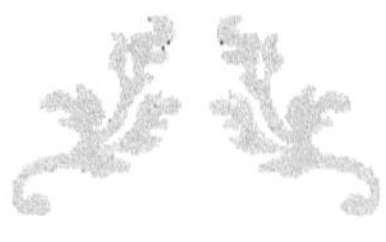

I was faced with the task of choosing who and what I was going to be from that point forward, not for anyone else, but for me.

Significance and belonging are both outcomes of relationships. I had a marvelous wife who had been waiting for 12 years for me to let her in so we could truly begin our relationship. Everything I saw in Kim and the potential of what we could build together, from the first day we met, was attainable. None of it was out of reach. It was just hidden and covered by many of the battles we had to endure along the way. It was always awkward when younger folks or other married couples would say to us that they thought we were a great example. They couldn't know what was lurking behind the façade.

My point is that I was already in the thing that was designed to give me what I was seeking all my life. Not that the relationship was going to fulfill me. I had to be fulfilled within myself first so I could bring that completeness to the relationship. What I didn't understand (that I do now) is that the relationship was designed for us to *relate* with each other. Meaning, we were on a journey together to help one another become the best version of ourselves that we could be as individuals and, therefore, exponentially greater together. All I had to do was stop hiding from the one who could help me all along and start seeking how we could move from where we were to where we envisioned ourselves being.

As I said before, marriage is simple. It is simply a choice to create a union and covenant with another individual where you both submit to and accommodate each other's needs. We are the difficult factors in the formula of marriage. The strategy is that if we can help fulfill each other's needs, then growth occurs in both of us. As that growth occurs, that is what becomes our focus. Therefore, whatever happened yesterday is minimized and simply becomes an experience—a source of wisdom. The joy and the excitement of submitting yourself to support your spouse and help them achieve their aspirations is so motivating that it becomes a big part of what you seek. In essence, there's no longer a need to look for belonging and significance because the two of you are redefining what that means and creating the perfect environment in which it can exist and thrive in a way that's customized just for the both of you.

If you're playing hide-and-go-seek, please understand that there is no place for that game or any other game in your marriage. Besides, your spouse will eventually find you. What they do when they find you will be strictly up to them, which defeats the reason you have been hiding in the first place. So, the way you win the game is to stop playing! Trust your spouse; they said they love you, so be transparent and expose them to the real you. Let them look at you for themselves; you'll be surprised at what they see. Speaking from experience, once you stop hiding and get transparent with your spouse, not only will they help you be able to stand stronger and taller, they'll give you that for which you have been seeking all along.

Chapters 5 & 6 Reflect Upon This

Accepting responsibility for our actions is quite humbling and sometimes a little embarrassing. It's easy to project and push the blame for our actions on those who may have identified and exposed the behaviors within us.

Now that you have done some self-discovery to identify your personality traits and resulting behaviors, reflect upon specific actions that you do as a result of that behavior. For example: If your behavior is being rude, think about what specific thing you tend to do to others that might contribute to limiting your relationships?

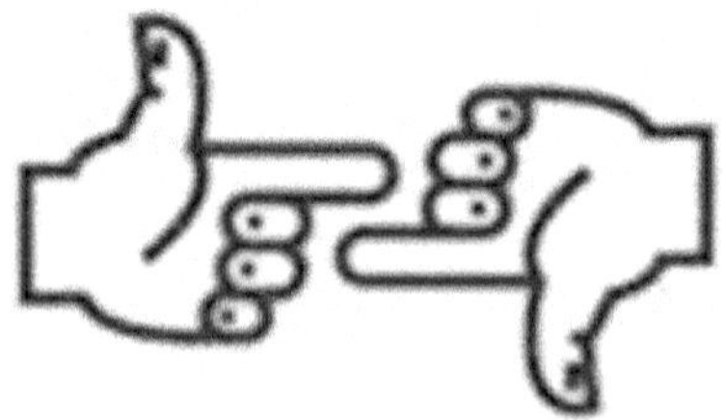

Chapters 5 & 6 Workbook Activity

Dear readers, tackling Activity #4 in the Baggage Claim Workbook is a pivotal step in understanding the intricate dynamics between your identified behaviors and interactions with others. By describing how the behaviors recognized in Activity #3 manifest in your relationships with others, you embark on a profound exploration of your social dynamics. This activity encourages introspection into how your behaviors influence and shape your interactions with friends, family, colleagues, and acquaintances. It prompts you to observe and articulate how your traits translate into actions, affecting communication styles, conflict resolution, empathy, and overall relational dynamics.

It is encouraged that you engage in Activity #4 as it is designed to empower you to recognize the impact of your identified behaviors on the quality of your relationships, offering a valuable opportunity for personal growth, self-awareness, and improved social interactions. Embrace this chance to gain deeper insights into yourself and your connections with others, fostering more meaningful and fulfilling relationships in your life.

7

Kim's Now What?

"After years of working to make it to this point in my life, the house was empty, and my void fillers were gone. Now, I had to face the person I loved who was also the person for whom my hope had depleted."

Chapter Seven – Kim's Now What?

Blurry Mirror

Facing problems while building a family is much more challenging than it seems, especially when both you and your husband are coming from two different worlds. When Newt and I compare the differences in our upbringing, it made perfect sense why life on Pacific Avenue (our first home) was so bumpy! The most important thing we can share with you about the meshing of our two families is that the children we brought together were amazingly beautiful! Yes, they behaved like growing kids, moving toward maturity while learning to understand themselves and dealing with two imperfect parents. Honestly, working with the unpolished tools that we gave them to use as they were growing up, I'd say, our children did a great job, with the tools they were given, and they loved each other regardless! I like to call them our little success stories. Each of them makes us smile every time we think of their unique personalities and gifts. Our kids were silly, loud, competitive, funny, talented, and truthfully, they were our friends.

The household we set up was far from perfect, but it was ours, and we loved every minute that we had to parent each of them and watch them grow. However, as you know, children aren't here to stay but are meant to grow and go; and that's what they did, one after the other. Every two years, we packed them up to drop each of them off at the college of their choice, and before we could prepare ourselves, we were empty nesters.

It was weird being in the house without all of the laughter, loud music, movies, or neighborhood kids hanging in the backyard playing on our little basketball court. Reality kicked in quickly, waking up in the morning in a lifeless, quiet house looking at Newt and he at me. We suddenly realized that all we had was each other. I remember when the kids were young, I was excited for the day that we would be alone. I looked forward to the freedom to travel and spend time together, especially since we spent most of our time working, finishing college, raising children, and celebrating their accomplishments. But now, the thing I had hoped for was staring me in the face, and I was empty!

After years of working to make it to this point in my life, the house was empty, and my void fillers were gone. Now, I had to face the person I loved but he was also the person for which my hope had depleted.

The truth is that I spent so much time being happily distracted by the little lives that I was responsible for, I spent very little time focusing on our marriage or what I needed. So, when the time came to give all of my attention to the marriage, I had very little hope in our future. I realized that I filled my emptiness and the void from Newt's absences (due to his personal struggles) with the needs of my children. After years of working to make it to this point in my life, the house was empty, and my void fillers were gone. Now, I had to face the person I loved who was also the person for whom my hope had depleted. When it came to Newt and trust, I was guarded, wearing the armor of protection. I had experienced so much disappointment during the earlier years of our marriage that I decided I would not allow myself to be hurt by anyone else ever again. So, Newt would have to take the lead to create change in the relationship, or we would end up going our separate ways. Until he could figure that out, I immediately found a new distraction and got busy focusing my attention on taking care of someone else: my mother. After my mother got ill, she and my sister took up most of my time, which helped me to keep my mind off of the problems in my home, heart, and with my husband.

To clarify, Newt and I did what we always did over the years of our marriage. We went to dinner, movie dates, bought each other gifts, and spent time talking, laughing, and doing whatever we could to make each other smile. Smiling was easier than addressing painful experiences. We were great friends, and we loved and wanted the best for each other. But for us to stop and address hurtful truths was too difficult, especially since neither of us wanted to hurt the other. But God has a way of allowing the controversy to stand up amid your busy life so that you have no other choice but to deal with the layers covering you! And the layers started to come off on their own.

For me, keeping busy has always been the way to avoid the things that were hurtful and difficult to face, and facing Newt was very hard for me at that time. Yes, I loved him, but I didn't want to watch him self-destruct. I was no longer willing to ride that roller coaster, so mentally, I got off this uncomfortable ride! Four months later, my mother died, and I was determined to rid myself of feeling sad, lonely, or any pain; so I decided not to mourn her death. As a child, I learned that crying was a sign of weakness. Running away from pain was the best way to deal with my feelings. So, I decided to relocate; I thought maybe if Newt and I left, we would forget all of the old memories of the past and make new ones. I believed that things would be different, or they would at least get better. But, at that time, Newt wasn't ready for that kind of change. So, I, being impatient at that time, packed my bags and moved to Virginia. I quickly got a job teaching fifth grade science, and I thought, finally, I'm on the right track for healing. But the plan that I had wasn't the plan God had for me. God has a funny way of redirecting you to the path of your purpose. So, four months after moving to Virginia, I was on an airplane to start the next phase of my life with Newt in San Diego, California; and my question was, "So now, what?"

8

Newt's Now What?

"The two people creating a functional household can love each other dearly. If they never deliberately feed and grow that love, then it will eventually take a backseat to what's being fed the most—the household and the reputation of the family name."

Chapter Eight – Newt's Now What?

Naked and Exposed

So, there we were, exposed and figuratively naked. I felt like I was standing in the middle of an open field with no covering, shelter, or protection from the elements; as if I was open game for any predator to jump from their hiding space, pounce on me, and have me for lunch. I felt as if I was standing in plain sight of a sniper who had me in his sights, positioned smack dab in the middle of their crosshairs. I was feeling lonely, unaccomplished, and embarrassed all at the same time.

I spent all of my time, talent and energy creating a functional household and neglected the work that I was supposed to be doing of creating a functional marriage relationship. I remember a couple who was married over 20 years, seemingly in a wonderful relationship, suddenly divorced and went their separate ways. When my wife inquired what happened, she learned that one of the partners in the couple had decided to hold things together until after their children had gone off to college. The shocking thing was that the individual kept those plans to themselves until the children were gone. But they were ready to leave too. That person did not communicate with their covenant partner and make them aware of the issues that were irritating them so much that they were ready to throw in the towel. So, there was no opportunity to create an environment where the couple could seek to understand each other more and commit to the work that would result in growth and resolve.

In essence, one of the partners had checked out of creating a functional marriage relationship many years prior and committed to settling for a functional household. Their children were raised well, went off to college, and are doing great things in the world today. Both the husband and the wife are fine human beings and have moved on with their lives creating new happiness. I used that example because, while in that marriage, things seemed fine to outsiders when they weren't. Now that the marriage is over, they appear to be doing well on their own. But are they?

Functional Household Versus Functional Marriage Relationship

Creating a functional household simply takes two individuals who are reliable and committed to making sure the bills are paid, comforts of the home are available, the children are fed and clothed, and a sense of morals, ethics, and values are upheld in the household. The two people creating a functional household can love each other dearly. If they never deliberately feed and grow that love, then it will eventually take a backseat to what's being fed the most, the household, and the reputation of the family name.

> **The two people creating a functional household can love each other dearly. If they never deliberately feed and grow that love, then it will eventually take a backseat to what's being fed the most, the household, and the reputation of the family name.**

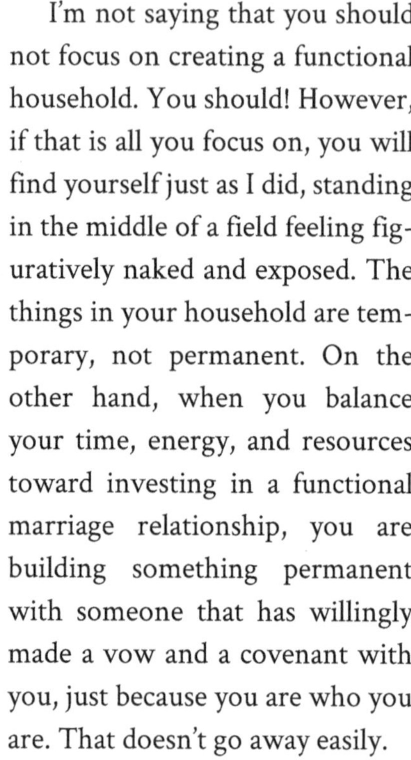

I'm not saying that you should not focus on creating a functional household. You should! However, if that is all you focus on, you will find yourself just as I did, standing in the middle of a field feeling figuratively naked and exposed. The things in your household are temporary, not permanent. On the other hand, when you balance your time, energy, and resources toward investing in a functional marriage relationship, you are building something permanent with someone that has willingly made a vow and a covenant with you, just because you are who you are. That doesn't go away easily.

All Gone

My father taught me that you don't raise your children to stay; you raise them to go. I would periodically repeat that phrase in our household, especially when there was a tense situation. Yet, throughout the years I made a gigantic mistake by investing in what was never meant to stay. In retrospect, I realize that I didn't understand everything the phrase was telling me to do. I thought it was simply reminding me to invest in our children so they were motivated and, in a position, where one day they could take care of themselves and not have to rely on us. However, that phrase was trying to tell me much more. It was telling me to pay attention to the one who is going to be standing there with me after all the smoke cleared and everyone was gone. The one who

I stood at the altar with and to whom I made vows before God and created a covenant until death do us part.

I spent a good portion of my time focusing on going to games, attending school events, doing science projects, talking about life, and pushing children in a direction so that they could have a lucrative and fulfilling future. With another portion of my time, I focused on attaining educational pursuits, so I could attain my career goals and increase my earning potential. With another chunk of my time, I worked long hours, volunteered for extra projects and positioned myself to move into leadership opportunities. I was thinking that it would bring more money into the household and make things easier. But what I did not know was that more of anything means more of everything. Whenever you get more of what you do want, you can count on getting more of what you don't want, as well. As I advanced in my career, I was pleased with myself and happy to make an impact in the lives of those I was leading. However, I never stopped to think about how those advances in my career, educational pursuits, and the time I was investing in our children was being subtracted from the time that I could have been spending with my wife. In essence, Kim was getting what was left over from everything else I had placed in line in front of her.

On top of that, throughout the years I developed some self-destructive behaviors that were at the root of some poor character choices that I was making. This meant that in addition to the positive things I was doing to pull time and attention away from building a functional marriage relationship, I had engaged in some negative behaviors which were pulling me away as well.

Now let's assume that you are not a knucklehead like me, and you don't have any self-destructive and self-medicating issues causing you to make poor choices, drain your resources, and pull time from your family. Even if you don't have any of those things going on in your life, the positive things you're doing could be creating an imbalance. This could be an indicator that you are focusing on building a functional household and not a functional marriage relationship. My point is that you have to redirect your focus to what is most important, and that is the person who will be standing there looking at you when all the smoke clears: your spouse.

Don't let things happen for you the way they happened for me. I came to a point when everything I devoted my attention to building was built. When all of the people, places, and things I used to make myself feel accomplished became things in the past, I realized that they were actually just hiding places. When all of the things I thought were so important in my life dwindled to afterthoughts such that I no longer depended on them, and they no longer depended on me, I had nowhere else to run and hide.

It was all gone, and there I stood, exposed and figuratively naked. I had been married to this person for many years but had no idea how to communicate with her when there was no one or nothing else around. It was all gone, and there we stood—no distractions and no hiding places.

Holding On to Nothing

Suddenly, I realized that everything I once used to establish my significance and sense of belonging had either grown up, moved on, or moved out. I felt as if I was slipping back down the hill of fulfillment. I had spent all of my time building a functional household and not a functional marriage relationship. When the things I was building did what they were supposed to do, I was left standing there with empty hands. As difficult as this is to realize, I had to admit that I created a false sense of significance around things that did not belong to me. Each of my children was born with his or her own purpose and had a life to live. My career was never meant to be permanent, and it was always subject to change. Besides, it was a result of my giftedness and my talents; my gifts were always meant to serve others, not me. My reputation was always contingent upon someone else's opinion of me. Therefore, it is not in my control and should not be one of my major concerns. None of these things ever belonged to me, nor were they in covenant with me and my well-being for the rest of my days here on this planet. Thus, my efforts to build a functional household included productive children, educational pursuits, and an influential career path. The irony is that if I had done all of those things correctly, what I was spending my time building was supposed to someday leave me standing alone. What I'm trying to say is, as you're building the components of your household, and you're doing them well, they're supposed to grow and go. They are supposed to mature and someday no longer need you the way that they once needed you when they were immature and in their infancy stages. I couldn't get down on myself because I had done a good job; I had accomplished what I set out to accomplish. I just didn't know that one day each accomplishment would leave me with empty hands, holding on to nothing but memories.

My wife and I had raised all of our children; each of them was sent off to college, had their own individual conversations with life, and were sustaining themselves. As life would have it, the covers were pulled off of me, and all of my poor character choices and negative decisions were exposed. There was no longer anything to hide in that arena. By now, my wife and I had separated, and what we had done such a great job of keeping private was also exposed. Therefore, there was no reason to spend time and effort to protect our reputations and attempt to filter how others may have thought of or reacted to us. At this point, we had to decide whether we were going to just let the chips fall as they fall and determine our destiny, or if we were going to hold on to what we had, take control of our destiny, and make our marriage work. The problem was, at least from my standpoint, there was nothing onto which I could hold. I didn't have anything in my hand because I had spent all my time building a functional household. I totally missed the priceless jewel that was staring me in my face all these years: my wife… my marriage relationship.

Memories – Blessing or Curse?

As any good mathematically-minded person would do, I began to analyze things. I began to organize my life and my marriage into categories or lists. I began to make a checklist in my memory of what I felt like I accomplished in the marriage in each of those categories or lists.

I began to think about what I had paid, what I had sacrificed, what I had brought to the marriage. Do you hear a dangerous pattern yet? I'm talking about "*our*" marriage, but I keep saying what "*I*" remember.

You see the problem with memory is that it belongs to us, and we can twist it and modify it to suit our needs. We can conveniently eliminate things, and embellish what we don't like, so we can justify to ourselves what we wanted to be true in the first place. That is exactly what I was doing. As you can guess, I began to harden my heart towards my wife and feel as if I really didn't need her at all. I didn't try to, but I'm sure I became dismissive and self-centered, and made her question whether I ever really loved her.

I was in full-blown Newton Miller mode, and I was ready to defend myself to anyone who sounded as if they believed I had any responsibility in the fact that my marriage was falling apart. My memory banks were telling me that I did a great job. I could hear myself whispering things in my own ear like: after all, look at all these other men who aren't even there for their children. They don't have half the stuff we do. I wasn't a cheater or an abuser. What more could she have asked for? These were the conversations that I would continuously have with myself to indoctrinate and justify myself. Looking back, I now understand that I was operating from my amygdala, my reptilian brain. Because I was reasoning from there, I was in fight or flight mode, and it was apparent that I was fighting to hold my pride intact. I just couldn't... No, check that... I just wouldn't come to reason with myself to realize that although the things I was remembering were true, I did not remember them correctly. I hadn't done those things by myself, and I couldn't, I didn't have the capacity, nor the ability. All the great things that I was remembering were things we had done together. If we hadn't been together, they probably would not have happened.

Nonetheless, I was in full fight or flight mode operating from my reptilian brain, remembering things how I wanted to remember them so I could justify what I wanted to be true, but clearly wasn't. In my mind, I fathomed that I was a great model of a husband, father, and human being who simply was not appreciated, and that was why we were in this mess. The reality of the matter was that I had spent all my time growing what was meant to go, and when it was gone, I had no relationship with my own wife. So now what!

Chapter 7 & 8 Reflect Upon This

When we identify a negative trait, we tend to operate in a fixed mindset and accept that it is negative now and forevermore. What if what has always been seen as a deficit is actually a gift?

We are challenging you to think of ways those traits previously labeled negative can be flipped upside down and be utilized in ways to positively impact your relationships.

Chapter 7 & 8 Workbook Activity

Dear readers, Activity #5 in the Baggage Claim Workbook presents a transformative opportunity to reframe and redefine the negative traits and behaviors identified in Activities #3 and #4. This exercise invites you to shift your perspective by renaming these traits as positive assets or gifts to others. By undertaking this activity, you embark on a journey of self-discovery and empowerment, recognizing that what might have been perceived as negative traits can be transformed into unique strengths and virtues.

Engaging in Activity #5 enables you to unlock the potential within yourself, turning perceived shortcomings into powerful tools that enrich not only your life but also the lives of those around you. Dive into this exercise with an open heart and witness the transformation of what once seemed negative into beautiful and valuable gifts you offer to the world.

9

Un-Arm

*"We must give each other space
and time to work our process,
to run our course, and be very
aware that the process and
course of our partner could look*

*very different than we expect it
to look."*

Chapter Nine - Un-Arm

H.O.W.

In a marriage, God has a funny way of taking each of you on two different journeys just to have your paths join back together farther along the originally intended path he had planned for you. I don't recall Kim and I ever saying this to each other, but I'm sure that while we were going through this phase of our journey, the same thought or something similar was rolling around in both of our minds... *After all that we've been through, and all that there still is ahead of us, if this marriage is going to work, the first thing we have to do is to unarm...*

Kim's Unarming Process - Part One

Bumpy Ride

My plane ride back to Newt was a bumpy one, and I found myself holding on tightly to the chair arms of the airplane. I was scared, and I thought, wow, if this airplane ride represented the life that Newt and I previously lived, then the bumpy ride was spot on! Nonetheless, I still chose to come and see if we were in a better position after dealing with our issues individually. During the plane ride, I asked myself, what are you going to do when you get there? Honestly, I didn't know! I kept telling myself not to do what I usually would by acting like everything was fine. That tactic only worked until I saw a glimpse of old behavior and allowed old feelings to be my mode of attack. I didn't want to be that person any longer. However, in my mind I was wondering if I knew how to forgive someone completely. My defense was like the items in the bags that I carried to school and could use at any time I needed to protect myself when I thought that Newt or anyone was trying to hurt me. So here I was on my way, afraid of the same things happening and also afraid of the changes that could be more painful. I had nothing in my bags to fight with because this new place was an unknown area that we never traveled. For the next 5 hours, a series of questions continued to flood my mind. Will you forgive and acknowledge your bad behavior? Do you have the ability to change so that you can save your marriage? My answer was yes to all those questions because I loved Newt with all of my heart, and I couldn't imagine my life without him. Honestly, I felt that it was more wrong for me to be without him; he was the other part of my life puzzle. I wanted our marriage to work, but honestly, I was scared! Since Newt asked me to join him in San Diego, I guess he also wanted it to work. I wasn't sure how we would start again or what Newt needed from me, but I thought the best place for me to start was to let the pain of the past go. I had to take responsibility for the part of the damage that I caused to our relationship, which meant I had to change ME! *So, I better hold on tight!*

Newt's Unarming Process – Part One

I Was the Key

Throughout the relationship, I was the one who had the outward and visible issues. I was the one making poor choices and engaging in self-destructive behaviors. Thus, throughout the years, I had developed a sense of guilt and shame. To protect myself, I built a wall so that no one could see those feelings. I could hide behind that wall and justify my actions by deflecting them on to others. The longer I hid behind that wall to survive, the higher and wider I had to build it.

One day, I was reminded of an old riddle that tells the story of a man who begins digging a hole. He digs and digs all day long until he gets tired. Suddenly, he realizes that he has dug the hole so deep that he is unable to get out. The riddle asks, "What is the first thing the man should do if he wants to get out of the hole?" Some people may say call for help. Others may say start digging steps into the side of the wall so he could walk out of the hole: and yet others may say begin to pile up whatever dirt is left inside the hole so he can climb on top of that dirt and walk out. All of these are great answers and will probably work, but they are not the first thing that the man needs to do. The first thing he should do is simply, stop digging! That is where my unarming process began. I had to "stop digging"! For me, that meant two things.

First, I had to forgive myself for the poor choices of my past and accept that the self-destructive behaviors that I once engaged in were things I did in a prior phase of my life, not *this* phase of my life. The reason I said I had to accept them was that they were real—they were true. Denying that they once were a part of my life was the very thing that had me caught in the cycle of chasing my tail in an unproductive place for so long.

Next, I had to take the momentum of that acceptance and forgiveness that I had given myself to begin dismantling the wall which I had been hiding behind for so many years. When I share with people the steps in the first part of my unarming process, they always question how I could forgive myself before accepting what I did. In their mind, they think it makes more sense to accept my actions before forgiving myself for them. In response, I simply explain that I was the one in my own way. I was my own worst enemy. I was my own opposition. Thus, to move past me, I first had to forgive myself. Thus I gave myself permission to face what I had done without paralyzing any progress that I could make by prejudging myself. I was the key!

Kim's Unarming Process - Part Two

Everything's Growing Here!

When I got off of the airplane, the first thing I noticed was a beautiful palm tree in the center of the airport and Newt waiting at the bottom of the escalator with a huge smile on his face. My stomach was doing flip flops! I was nervous and excited at the same time. It was funny. As soon as I saw his beautiful smile, I couldn't even remember anything that he did wrong. I was in love all over again, and we were back together again! We left the airport and started to drive towards our new apartment. I looked out the window and saw some of the most beautiful flowers that I've only seen at a florist or in a magazine, but they grew here in San Diego, my new home. I saw a Bird of Paradise growing from the ground, and it was one of the first flowers Newt bought me when we were dating. I told myself if our relationship was going to grow, then it was going to happen here because everything is growing here. *Wow, God, you're already showing me something new, and new was what I needed. Something that we never saw, felt or experienced before, something fresh, full of hope and excitement*—anything different to let us both know that change is possible! Experiencing new things with Newt was fun, but we could never get the full experience of this new life until we dealt with the unaddressed issues from our past. First, I had to realize that Newt's problems were his, and they weren't because I did something wrong. His childhood issues that surfaced in his adult life happened a long time ago before we met. Likewise, my trauma wasn't caused by him; these were problems that began when I was four years old. Although they took a long time to surface, they were the driving force that made me protect, defend, and fight back. But now it's all out in the open, and I don't have anywhere else to run in this new place. So, the only thing left for Newt and me to do is to grow because everything grows here!

Newt's Unarming Process – Part Two

Mentor

Now that I had broken the inertia in my unarming process by forgiving myself, accepting my actions, and dismantling my walls, I could begin eating fresh food. I didn't have to survive off the rations I had stored away behind my walls of guilt and shame. In essence, I could open the door and let someone else into my life with different ideas, views, and options for me to implement, so I could move from the place in which I had been stuck for so long.

This sounds like an easy task, but when you've been locked in a prison for so long and only partaking of the things that were available to you in that prison, those things become your norm. They define your standard operating procedure and create a culture by which you survive and exist. When those things change, what was once your foundation becomes tremendously unstable, and your life is now in a state of crisis.

As much as I wanted to communicate with my wife more effectively, I had to learn how to communicate all over again. This is where part two of my unarming process began. For me, that meant two things.

First, I had to humble myself. Keep in mind, to be humble doesn't mean that you think less of yourself or shrink yourself beneath others. It means that you are comfortable with thinking of others more often than you think of yourself, because you are secure in who you are and what you're capable of. At this point in my life, I knew that I was a very powerful young man, full of purpose, potential, and possibilities. However, I also knew that I was capable of royally messing something up. I knew this was true because, until this point in my life, my best thinking has done nothing but get me into trouble.

This brings me to the next step of part two of my unarming process. I knew that if I relied upon my own thinking, it wouldn't be long before I would find myself repeating the same cycles and recovering the same ground that I had traveled in my past. Thus, I had to find a mentor. To me, a mentor is someone to whom I give permission to tour every area of my life. That mentor had direct access to help me identify where my thinking, actions and reactions were looping me right back into the familiar territory of self-destruction that I had always known.

At first, I found temporary mentors in the thirty days of inpatient counseling work that I did. Then, mentoring was found in the one year of outpatient groups that I attended. Finally, I found a mentor in a pastor that had a very transparent, down-to-earth, and life-applicable online ministry that he called i.Church. The access to support, testimonies, study material, motivational messages, and other resources that this man had made available were exactly what I needed in my life. We are what we eat! As I began to dive in and partake of the things that Redemption World Outreach Center had to offer, I was unknowingly changing my diet. Thus, I was changing too. Faith comes by hearing, so he who has our ear tremendously impacts, if not controls, our destiny.

Apostle Ron Carpenter, the Senior Pastor of Redemption Church definitely had my ear and was influencing my destiny. I only met this man once, very briefly, at a marriage conference. I was more than impressed that he took the time to stop what he was doing and talk with me and accept a copy of my first book, "Why Some Seeds Don't Grow." I knew that I only had about 45 seconds, so I was unable to tell him how instrumental he had been in my life. He is my hero! He doesn't know it, but he has mentored me for the last twelve years of my life. The things that he has been gifted and purposed to do with his life have tremendously impacted mine. All I had to do was open myself to what he had to offer and be diligent and disciplined enough to do the work to implement the principles he was suggesting. As a result, I have experienced a more positive and prosperous trajectory in my life than I have before I submitted to a mentor.

Kim's Metamorphosis

Making changes after we began to address our issues was easier said than done, and we learned that quickly in the new Miller home. However, when we faced situations, we discussed the issues head-on, one problem at a time. But they continued to open past pains, which prompted us to look deeper inside of ourselves. Over the next few months, we realized that the only real way to grow up is to grow within, and that's what we did. Yes, there were tears, long talks, quiet days, and long nights, but we were determined! I started to look at the Newt I knew was there but never had the pleasure of meeting, at least until then, and it was my pleasure.

Nothing worth having is easy, and our reunion would be tried by fire. Newt and I started where we began—by becoming friends again. Understanding and respecting each other and allowing time for us to process helped both of us individually. I even began to mourn the death of my mother, which helped to remove blame from Newt, who was innocent, as well as any misplaced guilt from my own life. I didn't understand until I began to look inside of my own heart how the enemy, with my help, used a lie to devalue my self-worth and self-esteem; it even caused me to hate myself. Honestly, these were the things that kept me from being the amazing person God created me to be in the beginning. Because of that realization, I was able to unarm myself and move from defense to offense and get on the same team as my husband so we could play together. Now we're growing!

Newt and I relied heavily on a three-step process that forced us to be real about our feelings and our expectations for the relationship. This was how we kept ourselves on the same page and in an upward motion. By no means am I saying that we have mastered every issue of our rollercoaster life; however, we have successfully implemented strategies that have worked for us and believe that they are worth sharing.

H.O.W.

We have just shared with you the major steps in our process of unarming ourselves so that we can move from where we were in our marriage to where we could be. As you review those steps, you can see that Kim's process and my process were very

different. You know why? Because we are two different people. When God designed Kim, he designed her separately from

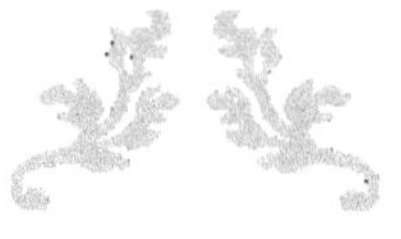

me, and when he designed me, he did so separately from her. Kim was formed through the intimate relationship that she had with God before the foundations of this earth, before she was even ordained in her mother's womb (Jer. 1:5); and the same applies to me. This means that we are two different individuals not only in our physical design, our emotions, will, and intellect, but also in our spirit man. This means that we must always allow each other to be who we are. We must give each other space and time to work our process, to run our course, and be

> We must give each other space and time to work our process, to run our course, and be very aware that that process and course of our partner could look very different than we expect it to look.

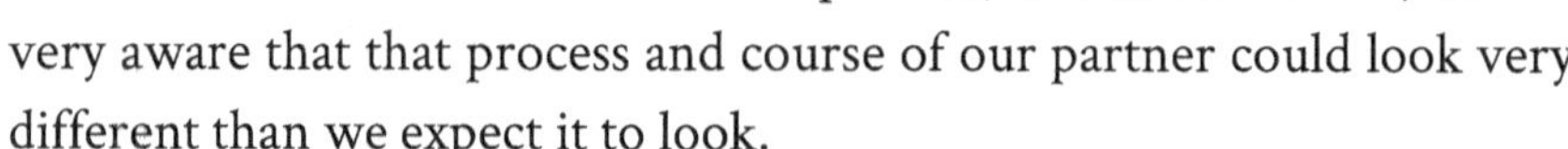

very aware that that process and course of our partner could look very different than we expect it to look.

No matter how different Kim's process was from mine and my process was from Kim's, there were three major components that engineered our unarming. You might be asking, well, how did you do it? H.O.W. is how we did it... At some point in our processes, we both had to be:

HONEST - with the good, bad, and ugly about ourselves;

OPEN - to input, suggestions and counsel from new sources that could provide different perspectives and options than
those with which we had become comfortable and familiar in the past years of our lives;

WILLING - to embrace constructive criticisms, input and suggestions, and do the work to implement them into our lives to
achieve a different outcome.

Newt's H.O.W.

HONEST

I got honest when I forgave myself, thus giving myself permission to accept the actions of my past. It was the brutal honesty that I confessed when I talked and thought about my past actions that began to permeate the shame and guilt that was blocking me from seeing who I really was. When I got honest about what I had done, how I was doing it, and why I was doing it, I took back my power. No longer could guilt and shame act as a mirror, only allowing me to see what was wrong, imperfect, and just downright ugly. When I got honest with myself, I stepped back into the driver seat of my life and was able to change directions. After all, what I had feared the most was exactly what I was addressing - myself. In my mind, admitting who and what I had allowed myself to become was the worst thing that could happen to me. Once that was over, and I was free to move on.

OPEN

The moment that I realized there was more available to me than what I had been allowing myself to be exposed to because of my guilt and shame, I became intrigued and open to what those things were. In my case, I happened upon Apostle Ron Carpenter from Redemption World Outreach Center, who was minding his own business, accomplishing his purpose from his corner of the earth. He was simply sharing resources, messages and instruction for how people could change to live a more fulfilled life by operating in their purpose. My spirit man knew that was exactly what I needed, and because I was living in honesty, my soul man knew it as well. So, I jumped in headfirst and began to partake of what he was offering. Although at that time, I had never actually met the man, I dismantled my walls and allowed him to tour my life by simply studying, meditating and analyzing what he was teaching. Once I became open to that new diet, my thinking, my attitude and my determination drastically changed.

WILLING

I discovered that once I was willing to apply the wisdom, experience, and counsel from one person in my life, it was easier to draw from the wells of wisdom from many other great people who had things to share with me. Now that my mind was open to alternate solutions, I had to find the diligence, develop the discipline and build the confidence to take on that new thing. At first, this was no easy task. It required me to retrain myself mentally and physically to speak and act differently than I had for the previous 40 years of my life. Being willing to implement principles in my life that I learned from one man began a journey of continuous improvement. Now, I continuously seek information and input from those who are where I am trying to grow.

Kim's H.O.W.

HONEST

Honestly, I was broken, and I was hurt. The pain I experienced was so deep that I couldn't pinpoint one person to blame; so, I blamed myself and everyone for what I was experiencing. Getting honest meant that I had to face myself by breaking down the walls to the protective force field I built so that no one else could hurt me. I got trapped in my own force field—trapped with negative words and lies that I fed and nurtured because I believed them myself. In my new walk of honesty, I had to learn how to face the trauma from my child-hood, and to pull it up by the root. This meant that if I wanted to be healed, I had to release the people who wronged me. I say release because, in my mind, I held them hostage; they were in one of the mental bags I carried around for years. In this honest place, I had to tell myself to let them go; this was one of the most difficult things I ever had to do. God knew I had no idea how to uproot something so large and so deep, so, he sent me to a church. There, a pastor by the name of Gwen Matthews began to ask me questions that were like a shovel digging into the area I was trying to unearth... and she didn't even know me! After attending this church for several months, I noticed a woman I had never met who was visiting. She stood up and said, "God wants someone here to know that the person who abused you is dead, and you will never get that apology from him, so God is saying it for you." The church was full, and no one budged. I stood there for nearly 5 minutes trying to convince myself that this message was for someone else and not for me. But the room was quiet and still, at least, until I walked in my truth and admitted that I was the person that the word was for. After acknowledging that I was the person, I felt free. Besides Newt, no one else knew that a few days before going to church, I was thinking about how this person will never be able to admit to or apologize for abusing me. So, when God sent this prophet to the church, I had to laugh because he was showing me that as I'm honest with myself, and him, he was going to take care of my broken heart!

OPEN

While attending this church, I met some beautiful people who spoke into my life. The words that God had given them for me were like ointment. I thought, *wow, someone finally sees me.* I had one particular young lady who attached to me; she encouraged me and spoke so well of me that at times I wondered if she was speaking of me. That was where I began to open myself to the real me. Pastor Gwen continued to tell me how beautiful, brilliant, and talented I was. She and her daughter, Victoria, were like a tag team, and they would not let me think anything negative about myself. They probably do not know how instrumental they were in getting me to the place of change. Pastor Gwen's nonjudgmental way of acceptance, forgiveness, and love helped me to see that the people who hurt me were also hurt themselves. They were simply repeating what they experienced in their own lives. Honestly, they needed as much love and compassion as I needed. The years that I spent at this ministry helped me to open my heart to be loved and to give love. Being open to receive and give love put me in place to forgive my husband completely and to love him unconditionally. This would allow Newt and me to be ourselves, and I really liked who we were together. I was open to accept people where they were, just like God accepted me. Learning that people are all important to God regardless of who they are and what they've done is the way I began to understand who God was, and who he wanted me to be. I was judgmental, and God was the opposite. At my church, I signed up for a course that taught me about the God I never knew - the one who loved, forgave, and accepted. I had been under the impression that God was mad at us and was waiting for us to do something wrong so that He could punish us. But I learned who God really is, and learning His precepts helped me to change mine.

WILLING

"Willing" happened when I made a decision to uproot everything that was an enemy to Him who was residing in me. This is a continuous process, and it is still in motion. I am learning every day how to use these principles to uproot any residue from the past. Being willing one time doesn't mean that the work is finished. No! It is a lifetime of application, and I'm still working on me. After I understood this method, I began to use it in everything that I did. When I fall short, I just start at the beginning being honest with myself, which opens me up to grace and a surrendered will. It all works together for my good.

Chapter 9 Reflect Upon This

As you begin to be more intro-spective about how you are im-pacting your own relationships, in what area in your life can

you be more Honest about your need for growth? Are you Open to receiving input, suggestions, advice, or counsel on ways you can grow? Most importantly, are you Willing to do the work necessary to realize that growth?

Chapter 9 Workbook Activity

You are invited to continue your journey through the Baggage Claim Workbook with Activity #7. This activity invites you to apply the H.O.W. (Honesty, Open-mindedness, Willingness) method to one specific trait or behavior that you and your spouse have collectively agreed to focus on. Through open discussions and mutual understanding, selecting a trait for this method signals a commitment to personal and relational growth. Embracing the H.O.W. approach allows for a dedicated and intentional effort to navigate and transform this trait into a positive asset.

By integrating honesty, open-mindedness, and willingness, you pave the way for constructive change, support, and collaboration within your relationship. This activity is a meaningful step towards strengthening the bond with your partner and fostering personal development. Seize this opportunity to utilize the H.O.W. method to cultivate positive change and witness the transformative power it holds within your relationship.

No Easy Task

"*I want to emphasize that learning to communicate effectively with your spouse where the two of you are the authority, and there are no buffers between the two of you, is no easy task.*"

Chapter Ten - 4R's

No Easy Task

While in the process of claiming our baggage to find out what makes us tick, we realized that we needed to un-arm ourselves to begin to communicate with one another. I'm going to be tremendously honest with you - that was no easy task! Dealing with your personal developmental issues while trying to develop a relationship with your spouse is flat-out tough to do. I'm reminded of the old saying, *You have to GROW up to GO up.* I now understand why that statement is said in that order.

As Kim and I reflect on the cycle of the communication process we encountered, we realize that it included four phases:

- Real
- Rough
- Recovery
- Results

As we describe the 4R's in more detail, it is our hope that you will learn to identify each phase of the communication cycle as it is happening—in real time—in your own conversations. When you become more aware of each of the 4R's, as they are occurring, you will be more capable of managing your own emotions so that you can respond to instead of reacting to your spouse.

Please understand that it took Kim and me years to learn to communicate effectively in our marriage. To keep it real, we are still learning. Even though we love each other, and we did some great things together, our communication process left much to be desired. I often wonder how much more accomplished and effective we could have been in raising our children and making an impact on the world together if we would have known the 4R's back in 1999 when we first got married. My point is, we are sharing these 4R's with you with the prayer that you would pay attention to them, sidestep potholes, and avoid roadblocks that are waiting to trip you up as you continue to walk your path together.

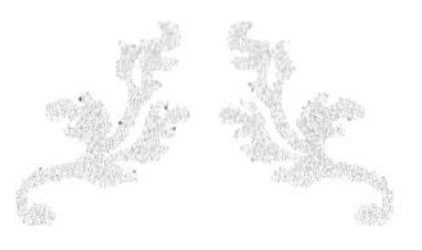

I just want to re-emphasize that learning to communicate effectively with your spouse where the two of you are the authority, and there are no buffers between the two of you, is no easy task.

I want to emphasize that learning to communicate effectively with your spouse where the two of you are the authority and there are no buffers between the two of you is no easy task. However, with a few simple tools, a committed attitude, prayer, and guidance from God, the two of you will continually draw closer. As a result, you will not only learn to only communicate effectively, but you will become one solidified, powerful, and productive unit.

The 4R's

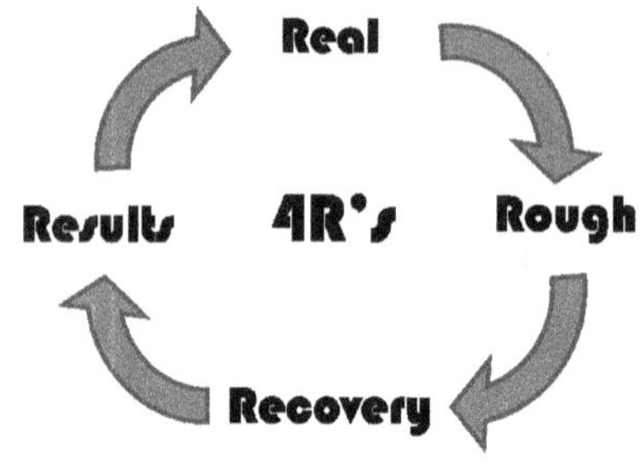

Marriage is Simple as P.I.E., but the journey is quite difficult. There are no easy ways to develop your relationship except through experience and training. Training yourselves with the tools to relate to your mate is a vital key to understanding them outside of selfish feelings and personal expectations. Through experience, Newt and I have developed a tool to promote a better way to communicate with your mate. We call it the 4R's of Communication.

REAL (Recognizing Everything About Love)

Speaking to your mate about your REAL feelings often triggers a reaction or retaliation out of a defense mechanism designed to protect themselves.

As an East coast girl, I grew up with the mentality that you tell it like it is! You speak your mind, and as long as you say what's on your mind and get your feelings off your chest, then you are good! My upbringing told me not to worry about how my words affected the hearer. For years, I lived my life thinking that releasing my words was cleansing my heart and removing the pain within. The funny thing about this process was that I never felt any better after spewing words out of my mouth. As a matter of fact, I found that, after each "mouth-pouring," I felt guilty and ashamed! It took me years to realize that saying what I needed to say wasn't the problem at all, but the spirit behind my delivery was what continued to cut me after I projected!

In this time of our lives, I've had to discover a new way to speak using R.E.A.L. words about R.E.A.L. issues that caused feelings, but to speak with pure love and compassion. This was difficult! How, in the Honest, Open and Willing way, will I be able to express myself with all of these bottled up feelings without an "I'mma get you" motive behind it? What I learned is you can do it through the same love and compassion you want when you're wrong! I started thinking about how much I loved this person and how I really didn't want to hurt him just because I was hurt! I started to give grace where I needed it. I didn't get it right all the time, especially since I had operated incorrectly for years; I admit that I had to repent and apologize often! But I was on the right track. I began coming to Newt as humbly as I knew; but his response was combative and defensive, and I didn't understand especially when my approach was kind and unintrusive.

I was being R.E.A.L. towards Newt, but I didn't prepare myself for Newt being R.E.A.L. towards me! One day, during one of my R.E.A.L. discussions with Newt about all of the things I didn't like that he did, Newt took the opportunity to share his R.E.A.L. opinions and views about my behaviors. This day was pretty interesting because Newt labeled a behavior that I never heard about myself; he told me that I was controlling! I thought my head was going to pop off. "Controlling?" I repeated.

He quickly responded, "Well yes! Whenever someone doesn't agree with you, you're upset."

I remember looking at him ready to respond immediately, but he gave me a few examples to back up his claim. I was upset, but I had to listen to what he said. The truth was that I had a problem being bossy and tended to command that things go my way.

Honestly, it was natural for me to be in charge being the oldest of eight siblings and the eldest grandchild. I hated what Newt said, and right away I felt defeated. It took me some years to admit my controlling ways, and although they were my norm since my childhood, it still didn't give me the right to usurp that authority on him or any member of my family. Sadly, I must admit that I did! I can't count the number of times I've apologized for my actions as I was confessing and learning how to change. This first step to better communication with your spouse is difficult, but it's all about keeping it R.E.A.L. with your loved ones as well as yourself.

Rough

Hearing the comments from your mate can cause feelings of rejection and judgment. These feelings can prompt a negative reaction and behavior towards your mate. This stage is when you field through all the rough terrain in an attempt to recognize the truth.

I'm not trying to be stereotypical or misogynistic in any way but in general, by design, men communicate a little differently than women. We tend to have this thing that gets in the way of our ability to freely receive during the communication process. We have no problem giving; it's the receiving that's unnatural for us. By design, we are meant to deposit seed into a receiver. Thus, it makes sense that receiving is a skill that does not come naturally for most men; we have to develop it. Not to create a graphic visual, but I'm sure that now you can see why I said that this truth is connected to our design as men.

I remember how rough it was for me when Kim and I were finally at the point in our relationship where we could simply put all of our "stuff" on the table. We weren't polishing it; we weren't considering how it was going to affect each other, we weren't trying to position ourselves to seem greater than the other. Nope, we just... put it on the table. Man, that whole process was particularly tough for me. What really got under my skin was that Kim seemed unmoved. She was a regular chatterbox, just flowing with words. I mean, from my perspective, she just wasn't stopping. If I would've copied down every-thing she said, I would've had about a 15-page paper! So, to say the least, at this point, I was struggling. There is a thing that many of us men carry everywhere we go called ego, and it has a first cousin named pride. The two of them were screaming so loudly in my ears that it was hard for me to receive anything that Kim was saying without immediately having something to say back. Like I said, giving was not my issue, receiving was.

One time, in particular, we were in a fairly heated discussion and I was feeling like I had all the answers. Just because I had accomplished a few things in life, I thought I was, "the man." Somehow, I had fooled myself into thinking that I was the standard and was outperforming people around me. Well, the conversation got rough when I was trying to elevate myself above a mutual friend by comparing what I perceived as his life accomplishments versus mine. Kim immediately responded to my criticisms by looking at me and replying, "He seems to be doing just fine, but look at the mess that you're in."

On another occasion, before I began to address my self-medication issues, Kim was upset with me - and she had a right to be - so she was telling me about myself. During that conversation she said to me, "The problem is you don't have any rules for your life." She went on to explain why she said that by listing some of the things that I had done and how I was seemingly okay with myself after having done those things.

I remember being angry, but at the same time in my head, I was saying to myself, "Yeah, she's right," and being embarrassed, all at the same time. I just didn't want to hear that about myself. For the things that pertained to myself, I had done what most men do. I had taken my poor choices, issues and feelings related to those things, packed them in a box, and put that box in a box. I then hid that box in the corner at the bottom of the closet, then put a whole bunch of junk on top of it so that it couldn't be found, and didn't have to be dealt with.

In hindsight, I can now admit that the "rough" phase of the com-munication process is what helped me to come to grips with how I was perceived by others and consequently, falsely perceiving myself. Don't run when it gets "rough." This is when you develop your giving and receiving skills which will make you a better communicator and draw you closer to your spouse at the same time.

Recovery

Recovery is only the halfway point towards change. Yes, you are closer because you've acknowledged some things, but old habits take time to break and change. Repair is also a painful stage in communication because it causes you to remember the how's and the why's that brought you to this point. Recognizing and addressing the hurts, struggles and disappointments of the past is the only way to full recovery.

After dealing with the real feelings and rough issues of phases one and two, you are ready to establish better communication with your spouse. You'll find yourself in the recovery stage where you have to accept what was said and how you felt about what was said. Then you have to be mature enough to commit to hearing your spouse's perceptions of you and submit to making a complete life change. Recovery is the place in your marriage where you pick up the valuable pieces that work to rebuild your relationship in order to make a beautiful puzzle. These puzzle pieces validate the needs of both you and your spouse in order to revive what was lost or internally hidden. In this phase, both of you will begin to see that your partner only has your best interest at heart. Both of our recovery phases were humbling because we knew that neither of us had any desire to hurt the other. The truth is that when you're being honest, you have to face areas of your life that are easier forgotten. Sometimes the transfer of words and emotions cause painful feelings to arise.

Results

At this phase, we create an action plan that includes tangible things that we can do to move forward and resolve our issues. Achieving positive results require us to choose to speak, react, respond, and think differently than before. It's here that we refocus and revive the relationship.

This is the phase of the communication process where you and your spouse have built some forward momentum. You have now realized that you both are on the same team, that you want the same thing and are working towards the same goals. Forgiveness has occurred. Keep in mind that forgiveness doesn't necessarily mean that the thing is forgotten. People leave things in your life and forgiveness is the first step that you take so that you can begin to release yourself from the thing that has been left. Now, releasing the thing still doesn't mean that you have forgotten it. It simply means that you have taken back control of your life so that thing is no longer an anchor or weight with the capability of holding you stagnant and in place, preventing you from moving forward with your purpose. In a marriage, it is imperative that we forgive one another so we can do the work to trust again, believe again, and progress again.

In the results phase of the communication process, we suggest that you create an action plan for what's next. Now that you've heard each other, you are at a point where you can communicate to meet each other's needs. We suggest that you write them down or put them in a place where you can review them daily and keep them at the forefront of your mind. The results phase is where you do what needs to be done to correct the problem or address the issue. The key is to make sure that the things you do to meet your spouse's needs in this phase, are not just the things you think they need. Make sure they are the things that your spouse has revealed in the Real, Rough, and Recovery phases of the communication process.

Throughout the years, there have been several times when my wife has sat me down and let me know that my actions made her feel as if I didn't love her anymore. In my mind, this was ludacris. I would often respond by saying things like, "Where else do I go? I'm always here," or "You know everything about me. My life's an open book. I have no secrets from you," or "We just have more responsibilities now, both growing and becoming more influential in the individual areas of our lives." The truth of the matter was I was justifying my actions because my time and my focus were on other things. As I gave my attention to accomplishing those other things, I was not giving my best time to Kim. Just so there's no confusion, Kim was not talking about negative things or poor choices that I was making. She was referring to the positive things that included responsibilities in my career, ministry, or some of the other areas that I was building in my life. At any rate, my actions were sending a message that Kim was not first in my life. So as a result, I had to step up my game.

Keep in mind, that Kim has communicated this need to me several times throughout the years, and I do not claim to have arrived and mastered that area, yet. As a matter of fact, I'm not sure if I ever will master it, but I have committed to doing all I can to meet that need.

After realizing that the 4R's is the pattern for effective communication, I was finally wise enough to ask clarifying questions to make sure I understood Kim's needs and expectations of me. I was then able to put them in a list and think about the things that I was doing that did not satisfy those needs and expectations. From there, I decided upon simple actions that I could do on a daily basis to meet my wife's needs. I chose simple things that would produce immediate and measurable results. She wanted me to respond to her needs, and I wanted her needs to be met. Here are several small things that I make sure I do on a daily basis to make sure my wife knows that I love her more today than ever before.

- Kiss her in the morning and say I love you, have a nice day before we go our separate ways.

- Text her sometime during the day to see how things are going.
- Call her when I know her day is wrapping up, or I know she is driving home.
- Kiss her when I come in the house.
- Ask how her day was and stop to listen (she usually beats me to this one).
- Tell her my plans, my goals, strategies, and ask for her input (She is my conscience).
- Make it a point to do something together each week, even if it is just to go walk and talk.

Chapter 10 Reflect Upon This

Understanding the cues for shifts in conversations can help you respond in ways that will help you be more productive.

Recalling a difficult conversation between you and your spouse, re-hash that conversation, not to relive the trauma, but to find where the conversation transitioned through each of the four phases of the 4R's.

What relationship limiting things do you recognize about yourself and your spouse when you phased into each of the 4R's as the conversation progressed?

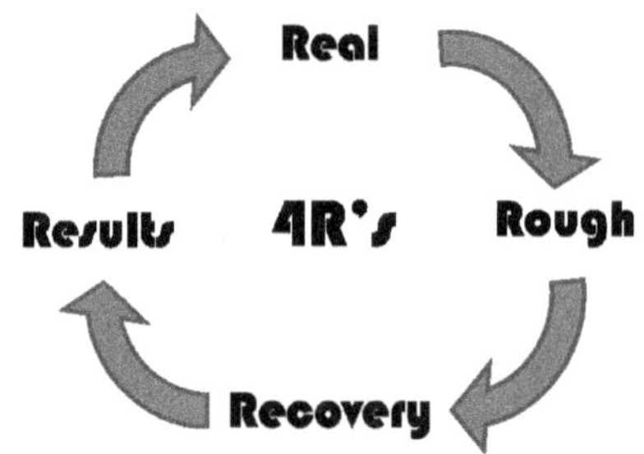

Chapter 10 Workbook Activity

Activity #8 offers a profound opportunity to enhance emotional intelligence and understanding within your relationship. This activity encourages you and your spouse to applying the 4R's methodology (Real, Rough, Recovery, Results) while revisiting a challenging conversation. This isn't about rehashing painful moments but rather about gaining insight into how conversations evolve through these phases.

By sitting together and exploring these phases, you gain valuable awareness of your reactions, responses, and emotional shifts during difficult discussions. Engaging in the 4R's method allows for a reflective exploration, promoting empathy, insight, and improved communication. Embrace this opportunity not only to enhance your emotional intelligence but also to fortify your bond by understanding and respecting each other's emotional journeys during challenging conversations. This activity serves as a cornerstone in building a more empathetic, supportive, and emotionally intelligent connection within your relationship.

The Art of Compromise

"...compromise is not about picking or winning battles or about what each person must give or take. It is about coming together to keep the promise that was made when the marriage vows were spoken."

Chapter Eleven - The Art of Compromise

Come to a Promise

At this point in our relationship, Newt and I had gotten to a place where we could really understand each other. It was hilarious—most times I could mime what Newt would say while he was saying it, especially if things were out of his organized space. He also knew what I would say if he were playing in my lotions or moving my jewelry around on my dresser. We were becoming one—in-tune and harmonious with each other's thoughts, feelings, opinions, and ideas. This only happened because we decided to disarm ourselves and work together instead of working apart. When we made that decision, it shifted our relationship to a new level. This newly added level was a needed flavor that seasoned our relationship. The ingredient was Compromise.

I know, you're thinking, compromise? I've always compromised in my marriage. Yes, you're right and I didn't think that this was anything new for me; but what I didn't understand about growing together was it also meant that as you grow up, you also go up. Growing up and going up means that you will experience similar things from the initial years of your marriage, but they will present themselves on a more in-depth level. For example, it will no longer be the bathroom light being left on or the empty juice container in the refrigerator that bothers you. Those previous things were juvenile issues with which we both had to learn to deal. However, this new level was more about our future, the vision for our marriage and the promises that we made on the day of our nuptials. This was no longer about getting to know each other as independent individuals; we had conquered that much, but now we were in the space of covenant. This new level pertained to the unchartered territory of our marriage. This territory addressed our mutual promise that would later yield mutual benefits. But what does it really mean to compromise?

No matter how much you love each other, it is impossible to be in a marriage and not have differences. Remember, you are two completely different people who are cleaving together to become one flesh. You were brought up in different households, exposed to different experiences, and before you met each other, probably had different goals, dreams, and aspirations.

When we became husband and wife, Kim and I didn't suddenly morph into two different individuals that had all brand-new goals, dreams, and aspirations. We brought our individualism to one single table, and the task at hand became blending that singularity to create one stronger, more purposeful and effective team. We quickly discovered that meant we had to learn to compromise.

Our definition of compromise is to simply "come to a promise." In other words, we wanted to make sure that together we could always accomplish what we promised each other we would accomplish. However, to do so we had to make sure our definitions of compromise were the same. As I'm sure you would guess, they were very different. As it turns out my definition was way more self-centered than Kim's was... Go figure! Remember, growing up I was the youngest in my family and the only boy, while Kim was the oldest of eight siblings. So, in my defense, it made sense that I was a little more self-centered... LOL. Actually, my point for bringing that up was to revisit an earlier chapter in the book where we talked about unpacking and claiming your baggage. Well, that was some of my baggage.

As we came to an agreement of what compromise or "come to a promise" meant for us in our relationship, there were three keywords that encompassed that meaning. They were "vulnerability," "sacrifice," and "submission."

Vulnerability

We learned that if we were going to ever "come to a promise" together, then we had to be willing to take risks - me in particular, since

I was the more self-centered one in the relationship. We had to accept the fact that we were in this relationship together and on each other's side. By design, Kim would often see things from a different vantage point than me and have different approaches. I had to learn that different wasn't better or worse. My responsibility was to take down my defenses and my need to control the situation. At first, this was difficult. I perceived it a risk to consider Kim's suggestions and different ways of doing things or finding solutions to issues. As I learned to be more defenseless toward her approach, simply because it was different than mine, I began to crave her input and found that the solutions we developed together were always much more productive than what I could come up with on my own.

Vulnerability is a good thing. It involves a choice to become powerless on your own, so you can become more powerful together.

Sacrifice

Sacrifice (or the lack thereof) was a huge hindrance in our home for many years. Simply because I, not Kim, did not fully understand what it meant. Sacrifice is not fair; it is equitable. This means that Kim and I both sacrificed in our marriage based upon our own ability to do so. For example, there were times in our marriage where I made more money than Kim, so my sacrifices towards the finances of the household were greater than hers. However, there were times when Kim made more money than I, so her financial sacrifice to the household was greater than mine.

I was blessed with a wife who taught me that the situation or circumstances we met in our marriage were just that - our situations and circumstances. Whatever we went through, we went through together. Kim would say that we should both always aim to give our reasonable service in our marriage, with the understanding that what's reasonable for each of us may not be equal, all the time.

I'm sure you've heard or maybe have said that things should be 50-50 in a marriage and two halves make a whole. Here's the problem with that philosophy: if both partners only give 50% to the marriage, they are only giving half of themselves to their covenant. So, if we're always aiming to give 100% to our relationship at all times, then our individual sacrifices are reasonable and based upon our ability; and that is something with which we should both always be comfortable.

Finally, we urge you to be investment minded within your marriage relationship. This means that whatever you give to your marriage is really not a sacrifice, it's an investment. It's an investment in a thing that you're growing. It's an investment in your product, the foundation of your legacy that will define not only the quality of life that you and your wife will live, but how your children and your children's children will live. This means that there are no tally sheets in a marriage. I always cringe when I hear people say we need to go 50-50 in our household. To me, you're setting yourself up for failure because you cannot always guarantee equality, but you can always strive for equity. So, throw out the tally sheets, stop keeping score in your marriage!

Everything you do in your marriage should be approached with the expectations that you are investing in each other and a win-win will always be the outcome. Besides, every sacrifice that you make in your marriage teaches and enables your spouse to grow into an individual that's more sacrificial minded. Thus, the more you invest in what you're building together, the greater your marriage will be.

Submission

This word can easily turn women off. Mostly because it has been used to give permission for someone else to be in control of making decisions for your life. However, the correct understanding of submission is completely different. It's funny, but as a young wife in my first marriage, that definition was my understanding based upon the teachings I received years ago. So, in an effort to reach you and not preach to you let's look deeper into the roots of the word. Let's start by breaking the word "submission" apart. *Sub* means to plunge and function under. *Sub* also means to stand in proxy as a representative of someone. The word *mission* means to see, accept and understand the calling, vision, ideas, plans or goals of one. In other words, submission means to stand under and support the vision or plan for the family regardless of who has the idea. This is done at will and not by force! It means that both husband and wife accept what the other brings to the table and are willing to comply by consenting to what works best for the family. **Understanding** or **"under-it -I-stand"** means to *stand under* the vision of your spouse, not sit down or bow under them.

For us men, whether we are believers or not, we always tend to point back to the verses in the Bible that say, "wives submit to your own husband..." (Ephesians 5:22) and, "husbands love your wives as Christ loved the church..." (Ephesians 5:25). We look at those verses and say, "That's right, it's in the Bible; you need to submit to me." Hold on a second; Kim just very eloquently showed you that the definition of submission means to be under the mission of a thing, which implies that if you don't have a mission, then there is nothing for your wife to stand under.

My point is that Christ loved the church in a sacrificial way. He submitted to the death of the cross for the church to take root, grow and thrive into its full potential. So, when we are told to love our wives as Christ loved the church, it implies that we (husbands) must first submit to the greatness that is in our wives. In other words, we must become submissive to the responsibility to protect, invest and empower that greatness and potential that exists in our wives. Our end game should be to do what it takes to help them get into position so they can operate in and maximize their purpose. Afterall, isn't that what Jesus did when He chose to sacrifice His own life to ensure the birth and sustainablity of the church? When we submit to building and supporting the greatness, purpose and potential in our wives, they will align that potential to provide the fuel necessary to accomplish the mission to which we have committed.

"God said, it is not good that the man should be alone..." (Gen 2:18a), so Eve was created. This means that Eve was an answer to a problem, a solution to an issue. My brothers, she was not created to serve you and your needs and desires, Eve was created so that Adam could accomplish the tasks that God had set before him in the garden. Thus, the scripture Genesis 2:18b, "...I will make him a help meet (suitable) for him," means, here is one not only who can help you, but is suitable to help you accomplish the things that I (God) require of you. This teaches us that woman is not less or greater than man, just different. In fact, she is different by design in order to make sure we (mankind) are capable of fulfilling our purpose of furthering the kingdom of heaven here on earth.

Because of woman's original purpose, we men were told to love our wives. However, we cannot love someone unless we are first submissive to their purpose. I said all that to say this; submission is a two-way street. If we submit to our wives by loving them, they will openly and honestly communicate with us so together we can derive a productive plan or mission for our marriages. Do not be deceived, neither of you are exempt. At some point in your marriage, you are both going to have to submit your immediate will to the greater vision or mission for which your marriage stands. Our commitment to display our love, respect, honor, and servitude to our wives is the very definition of submission. To submit means simply to commit. In other words, you get what you give.

Seven Keys to Compromise in Marriage

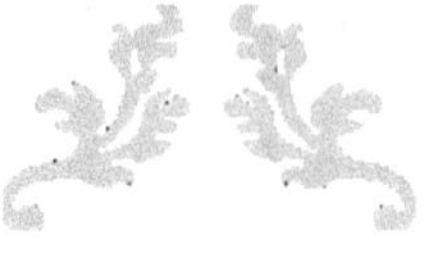

> ...compromise is not about picking or winning battles, or about what each person must give or take. It is about coming together to keep the promise that was made when the marriage vows were spoken.

Compromise or *coming-to-the-promise* together is vital in any relationship, whether it's with co-workers, friends, or family members. However, it is especially essential in the most important relationship in your life - your marriage. It is important to know that compromising in a marriage is meant to ensure that a win-win result is achieved as a collective outcome. This means that in a healthy compromise, the whole marriage relationship must be the focus, not singular interest of individuals in the marriage. This is important for both husband and wife to understand; so, when the need for compromise calls for one of them to maintain a position, it is not a self-centered stand. It is being done to enhance the marriage relationship for everyone involved (husband, wife, and family members). By the way, this can only occur if partners in the marriage have an element of trust in one another; not trying to gain advantage in the marriage, but to advance the relationship.

When this is done, compromise is not about picking or winning battles, or about what each person must give or take. It is about coming together to keep the promise that was made when the marriage vows were spoken. When done correctly, the process of compromising or *coming-to-the-promise* should be something to which husbands and wives look forward. It is an opportunity to work together to solve a problem; and to make the life-long journey more empowering and enjoyable for each other.

Check out these seven keys to conducting a healthy compromise in marriages.

Don't always try to be right

The biggest problem with disagreements is that each person *wants to be right*. Everyone likes to win... that's human nature! Although it is understandable, it is a position from which we must train ourselves to view differently. When an individual wants to win a disagreement, they are only focused on making their own point. They are usually not listening to any of the considerations that are important to their spouse. There are two sides to a conversation; so when we suspend *our need to be right* and choose to actively listen to each other, everyone wins.

Let things go

We are all human, and in our marriages, we will eventually do something that requires forgiveness. Forgiveness is the act of *giving forward grace.* This means we must release each other of past wrongs that have affected us. However, keep in mind that it is highly probable that our spouse will inadvertently do something in the future that may be a source of new consternation. Just because they did something that rubbed us wrong a few weeks ago doesn't mean it's relevant to any present or future challenges we may encounter. Learn to let things go.

Re-think your desired outcomes

Have you ever been in the middle of a disagreement and halfway through realized that the issue that has caused you to dig in and refuse to be flexible is not as important as you are making it out to be? It's tough to admit, but even after realizing that it is not that important, many of us will not change our position to a more flexible one. A powerful strategy we can employ is to be aware of our emotions so that we can keep them in check. This allows us to keep the bigger picture of what we want from our relationship in the front of our minds. That larger goal helps us to instantly re-think the desired outcomes we are aiming for from the difficult exchange in which we are presently engaged. There is nothing wrong with asking yourself, "Is it important that I dig in so firmly or will it be fine if I adjust my expectations. This key is applicable in all the relationships in your life. In difficult situations, re-thinking what will be considered acceptable to reach the desired outcome will relieve stress and increase productivity in your marriage.

Show that you are willing to change

It is one thing to re-think your desired outcomes, but it is another thing to adjust those expectations. Key number four to healthy compromises in marriage is to be willing to act on those desired outcomes that you have just re-thought. A major part of compromising is showing that you are willing to follow through with what you have promised. Show your husband or wife that you are completely willing to come-to-a-promise together. This way they will know that you are committed to moving forward to a better place in the relationship and not just making false promises to end an uncomfortable disagreement.

Share your thoughts, feelings, and beliefs

Compromising is about coming-to-a-promise together. The key operable word, in this case, is *together*. It is unwise to abandon your thoughts, feelings and beliefs just to be seen as a great compromiser. This will only plant seeds of resentment and cause bitterness. A healthy process of compromise demands that each partner expresses their thoughts, feelings and beliefs about every situation. This means both partners must be Honest, Open and Willing (H.O.W.) with what is going on internally that is causing a need to compromise. One strategy to accomplish this clear and honest dialogue is to utilize "me" and "I" statements when communicating. This makes it clear that what you are communicating is how *you* feel, and it is okay if your partner feels differently. The goal is not to force your feelings or opinions on your spouse; it is to create a culture where it is safe to express what is happening inside of you. Remember your spouse *loves you*, so knowing what is happening inside of you is important to them. Sharing your thoughts, feelings and beliefs as issues arise in the journey of marriage will make coming-to-a-promise together easier and more meaningful.

Appreciate your partner's efforts

Always, and I mean always, let your husband or wife know that you appreciate their efforts to come-to-a-promise. Being willing to compromise, instead of digging in and refusing to budge is a testament of your spouse's love for you. Not only is that an admirable trait...that's what you want, isn't it...just to love one another? Show your husband or wife how much you appreciate them for working with you to find the best solution. A strategy you can employ to show your appreciation for one another is to take time together to deliberately evaluate the outcome of the compromise. Make sure to highlight and express how much you appreciate and enjoy the positive social interaction you just had working together. Emphasize how it energized you and made you feel even closer to them.

Remain open to doing it all again

Keep in mind that it most likely will be necessary to come-to-a-promise again in the near future. Therefore, remain open to doing it all again. Just because you made it through the process of compromise once, does not make it an automatic and mechanical behavior. In other words, it could very well be difficult each time you have to come-to-a-promise. Keeping an open mind, being willing to change your expectations, not trying to be right in the first place are all powerful keys to compromise in marriage. However, you must remain open to working through the process every time it is necessary for you and your spouse to come-to-a-promise. Each scenario and situation you face is unique and deserves your undivided attention and effort to remain open to doing it all again.

Compromise Navigator

This compromise navigator provides suggested steps and supporting questions to navigating a compromise in a marriage. Although we recommend that you utilize all the steps presented on this compromise navigator, you should pick and choose what supporting questions and thoughts best fit your particular relationship, scenario and situation.

Step One

Review the Seven Keys to Compromise and ask yourself and your spouse these supporting questions:

- Which of the seven keys do you think will be most challenging for you or your spouse?
- What are some things you are going to do to ensure that you adhere to the seven keys?

Step Two

Verbally agree that you will do your absolute best to apply the Seven Keys of Compromise before you begin your discussion.

Here is a supporting statement you can use to show that you are committing to the *"come – to – a – promise"* process:

- I agree to do my absolute best to apply the Seven Keys to If by some chance I am not applying one of the keys, as my partner,
- I give you permission to keep me on track with reminders.

Step Three

Choose who will speak first and let them finish expressing their thoughts, feelings and position BEFORE responding.

Here are some supporting thoughts and questions you can ask yourself to ensure that you do not interrupt your partner:

- Take a step back and tell yourself, "Although what my partner said jolted me, it is not enough to stop the whole process."
- Listen with the intent of hearing all the facts of the situation from your partner's perspective by asking yourself these questions:
    - How does it impact them?
    - What might they be feeling?
    - What are the most important things to extract from the conversation?
- Be sure to use "I" statements as you share your thoughts, feelings and beliefs about the situation. At this point in the game, the only finger that you're pointing should be at yourself.

Step Four

Respond to what your partner has just said not to present rebuttal, but to make your thoughts, feelings and beliefs known.

Here are some supporting thoughts you can keep in front of you to ensure that your response is as productive as possible:

- Keep in mind that at this point it is not about winning an argument or trying to prove who's right and who's wrong.
- You are simply placing all the information on the table so that two intelligent adults who love each other can have enough information to make an informed decision that benefits the relationship.

- Respect is key… Both of your thoughts, feelings, and beliefs about the situation are equally valid. Do not in any way disrespect, disregard or devalue what your partner has just shared with you in your response to them.

Step Five

Offer solutions to the situation and tell why you believe the solution you're offering is a good one.

Here are some supporting thoughts and questions you can ask yourself to ensure that you communicate the possible

solutions that you're proposing in a way that they can be received by your partner:

- All solutions proposed must support the overall goals of the relationship, not the advantages of separate individuals in the marriage.
- Share with your partner what you've learned about them in the relationship. Explain why you feel the solution thatyou're proposing is considerate of the responsibilities that they may have outside of the marriage (work, family, church, community-based commitments, etc.).

  Ask yourself these questions:

  - Is the solution I am proposing good for the long run of the relationship?
  - Am I truly considering my partner's feelings or is the solution I am proposing self-centered?
  - Will this solution jeopardize any of the concrete plans around finances, real estate, or other investments you are working towards in your marriage?

- Does this solution require my spouse or me to compromise any of our core values?
- Does this solution support what I know to be my spouse's future dreams, goals and aspirations?
- Does this solution require my spouse or me to stop communicating or limit our social networks with close friends or family who are positive influences in our lives?

Step Six

Both partners must agree to the plan and verbally restate it to each other to ensure that they are on the same page and agreeing to

the same thing.

Here are some suggested ways for you to conduct the *restating step* of the process. Say to your partner:

- What we agreed to do is…
- What I think we have just agreed to do whenever this situation arises is…

Step Seven

Tell your husband or wife that you appreciate their willingness to "come – to – a – promise" with you.

Here are suggested messages that you could communicate with your husband or wife to show your appreciation:

- Tell your spouse that you appreciate how in love you are with one another and that you can communicate so productively even when the topic is difficult.
- Tell your spouse how much you appreciate solving issues with them.

- Tell your spouse how much more you trust them because of your ability to communicate so openly and freely withone another.
- Tell your spouse how coming – to – a – promise together has made the relationship stronger than it ever was before.
- Thank your spouse for being flexible and focusing on doing what's best for the relationship. Re-assure them that you know that what you have agreed upon may not be the easiest thing for them, but that you love them for doing what's best for the relationship as a whole.

Again, we recommend that you utilize all the steps presented on this compromise navigator. You should pick and choose

what supporting questions and thoughts best fit your particular relationship, scenario and situation.

Chapter 11 Reflect Upon This

The keys and compromise tool combines the "7 keys to Compromise," and the "Compromise Navigator" into a powerful at-a-glance tool. This tool can use used individually or together before, during, or after a conversation.

Which steps or keys will be difficult for you to implement? What can you do to make them easier to adopt? How much easier will it be to communicate in more focused, healthy, and productive ways.

Chapter 11 Workbook Activity

Since you desire to create deeper connections within your relationship, Activity #9 in the Baggage Claim Workbook presents a great opportunity to explore and resolve differences constructively using the Keys and Compromise Tool. This activity encourages you and your partner to select a topic where differing opinions exist, and then, utilizing the Keys and Compromise Tool, navigate the discussion toward a positive resolution.

This amalgamation of the 7 keys to Compromise and the Compromise Navigator offers a structured yet flexible system, fostering a productive and solution-oriented conversation. By embracing this tool, you pave the way for respectful dialogue, understanding, and effective compromise. Engaging in this activity isn't just about resolving differences; it's a testament to your commitment to mutual understanding and respect within your relationship.

Embrace this opportunity to navigate disagreements with grace, empathy, and a shared goal of finding common ground. The Keys and Compromise Tool serves as a guide, facilitating a productive conversation that can lead to a positive resolution and strengthen the foundation of your marriage relationship.

12

P.I.E. & PI: Finding the Right Formula

"God ordains marriages, and each union is unique and different. Marriage does not have a "one size fits all" formula that works for every relationship. Instead, it takes a specific blend of maturity and sacrifice that work together and, like a fine wine, are developed over time."

Chapter Twelve - P.I.E. & PI: Finding the Right Formula

P.I.E.

Over the last 11 chapters, Newt and I have taken you on a journey by sharing many of our stories. We have also provided steps that helped us build our marriage, which is far from perfect. To be honest, every step was challenging and at times downright difficult. But that's to be expected since there's no one-size-fits-all template to produce a perfect relationship. If there were such a template, there would be no problems or divorce in any relationship. Since that's not the case, it's simple; each of us has to work on the right formula to fit the needs of our unique marriage. The ingredients that made our marriage grow can only be a guideline to help each of you understand the importance of building your own relationships. So, to support your endeavors we came up with this simple acronym of **P.I.E** which means you must **Provide** for, **Invest** in and **Empower** each other in your marriage. These three words have been the guide to our understanding that **MARRIAGE** is just as **Simple** as **P.I.E.**

Provide

To many, the word "provide" means to make sure that the necessary supplies to exist are in place, such as clothes, food, and shelter. Kim and I have discovered that the word "provide" is much deeper than securing essentials. The word provide has two distinct syllables: "pro" and "vide." According to Merriam-Webster Dictionary, the prefix "pro" refers to a precursor, front runner, earlier than, or prior to. It also means to be in favor of or to champion or support. The second syllable "vide" is the root of the word "video" which means "to see." When you put the two portions of the word back together, the word provide means to see a thing prior to it occurring in order to support or champion that thing.

In essence, Kim and I have learned to *provide* or become a guide and a light for each other. We operate in the expressed purpose of helping one another to see, plan and prepare to accomplish both our individual and collective purposes and goals. Coming to discover what "pro-vide" really means has enhanced our ability to support one another and communicate more effectively. Knowing that Kim is always going to be looking ahead on my behalf and that I will be looking ahead on her behalf makes it easier for us to make adjustments as individuals in pursuit of purpose. It also keeps us aligned with the fact that we are a team and that we are continuously crafting and pursuing the vision of our collective purpose TOGETHER!

Invest

To invest in one another means exactly what it says… To invest in one another. This is difficult for people who may have spent any portion of their lives in socio-economically distressed conditions. Those of us who have experienced those conditions tend to operate in a survival mindset. This means that we are always focusing on just what we need to survive for the moment. For people operating in this mindset, this is just the way they live and it doesn't sound like a problem until you begin to grow a thing from the concrete position in which it exists to an abstract idea that can't be seen or touched yet, only spoken of.

The survival-minded person is usually unwilling to let go of the concrete things that they know have helped them exist and survive. After all, this is all that person has known and depended upon. Thus, it is very difficult for them to release what they know for an idea that is still developing or a possible outcome that is not yet producing any returns. They are unsure whether that idea is enough to sustain them so they can simply survive. I guess I don't have to tell you that this reaction or resistance is rooted in a very real place of fear. The survival minded person will make choices based on the reasoning that "a bird in the hand is worth two in the bush." Thus, they will not let go of one thing to reach for another. To them, letting go is a sacrifice, and the words sacrifice implies deficit or loss.

Kim and I have learned that in our marriage relationship there are no sacrifices, per se. Everything that we give to each other, or to what we are building together individually or collectively, is an investment—not a sacrifice. Sometimes what we give may be inconvenient or uncomfortable. If I'm perfectly frank, it can set us back a little financially or emotionally. However, throughout the years, what we have experienced is that, whether it be time, talent or finances, the returns on our investments in each other have always reaped bountiful harvests. I want to pause for a moment here to refer you to our children, all of whom are productive and impactful, and our nine living grandchildren who are all healthy, safe, and being raised in households that are speaking possibilities into their lives. I could talk about the material things and properties we own, the careers that we have worked together to establish, or the many lives that we have been blessed to influence both individually and collectively. Referring to those things is not an attempt to boast or brag, it is a direct reflection of the result of what Kim and I have invested in each other. What is really exciting to me about the investments we have made is that we have seen only a small portion of the returns. The best is yet to come!

Empower

One thing I think Kim and I were always great at doing for each other was empowering one another. Merriam-Webster Dictionary defines "empower" as the ability to influence someone to self-actualize a vision which they have the authority to accomplish. From the day Kim and I met one another, the empowerment process began. I didn't know this then, but I know it now. The ability to empower other people and motivate them to operate in their purpose is part of our individual inherent designs. It is something God placed in us before time, when he was forming us for our purpose on the planet. So, it makes sense that once we met each other, we would begin empowering each other as individuals.

When I met Kim, it was a transitional time in my life. As I began to share some of the pain points I was experiencing, I remember that she didn't blink or budge, nor was her immediate response to coddle or baby me. Instead, she validated my existence right where I was. She spoke into me in a motivating way to encourage me to get up from where I was and press forward because there was still some work to be done. If that's not empowering, then I don't know what is!

I remember when Kim shared with me that she wanted to be a teacher. At that time, she had not even begun her bachelor's degree, and we were in our 30s. My response was simple… "Go to school and be a teacher!" There was an awkward four or five seconds of silence as she stared at me with a look in her eyes as if to ask, "Was it really that easy" I explained to her that the higher education industry is a business that makes money when you enroll in their programs. I reminded her of all the things that she was already doing, working with young people to enhance their lives, and why wouldn't a university want to be the one to get her credentialed as a teacher so she could affect even more lives. The very same night, Kim was enrolled in college and taking her first class. Motivating, isn't it!? That is how you empower!

Did she immediately fix the problems and issues I was experiencing and shared with her when we first met? No, she did not. Did I take her by the hand and drag her to the college and fill out the applications and the FAFSA, and register her in her first courses? No, I did not. However, we provided each other with words of support and actions to back up those words that motivated each of us to move from where we were to the point of accomplishing the goal that we were communicating.

In essence, we engaged in an on-demand process of empowering one another.

I have observed many husbands and have made a general observation that we men tend to think that we have to dictate the path of our wives' lives. That is simply not true! As we stated in an earlier chapter, we were each created individually with a purpose of our own. By design, male mankind needs female mankind in order to accomplish what is set in front of us as the total mankind, and vice versa. So, husbands, man to man, I encourage you to get out of your wives' way. Engage them in conversation and listen intently so you can create a mental picture of what they said and what they want to accomplish. Then, it becomes your job to be like Adam and "till the garden." Your responsibility is to do the work to support your wife so that she is influenced to self-actualize that which was already in her to accomplish.

Needless to say, wives, you must do the same for your husbands. Not to let husbands off the hook, but by design, it's a whole lot easier for you to empower us than it is for us to empower you. God made you wo-man (man with a womb), so you have an ability to incubate and grow things that we men do not. So be a little patient with us as we learn what it means to and how to empower you. Quiet as kept, when it comes to empowering, you are the teacher, and we are following your lead.

I said all that to say that when we as husband and wife empower one another, it doesn't matter who outside of our relationship is for or against us. When we know and are confident that we are on each other's side and have each other's backs, there's absolutely nothing that can hinder us from performing that which we set out to accomplish.

In summary, you both must, **Provide** for, **Invest** in, and **Empower** one another (P.I.E.).

PI (π)

According to Merriam-Webster Dictionary, the symbol π, pronounced PI, is the ratio between the circumference of a circle and its diameter. It is also known as an irrational number whose decimal never repeats. The value of PI is (approximately) ≅ 3.1415929..., where the values of the decimal places continue on forever and never repeat their sequence. I know what you're saying... this is a book about marriage; why is he going into a math lesson? Well, it's simple: PI is a ratio between circumferences and diameters of circles, and every circle can potentially have a different circumference and diameter, therefore a different ratio. Also, the decimal places in the number PI go on forever without repeating any particular sequence. Do you get it yet?

In mathematics, we use PI, which is a steady and accepted concept, to bring stability and consistency as we calculate the values of things that could be very different if we compare them item by item. For example, we use the same formula to calculate the area of a circle even though each circle is very different. PI adjusts that formula ever so slightly to account for the differences in each circle. Your marriage is the same way. You have to adjust information you receive to account for the differences in the pieces of your formula.

Kim and I can tell you principles, share with you our mindsets, and tell you what we think worked for us in the process we went through, in order to come to grips with ourselves so that we could better communicate and relate with one another. You could listen intently, take notes, and apply to your marriage step-by-step exactly what we implemented in ours. Although it would be flattering, we guarantee that you will not get the same result that we did.

Although there are some consistencies and great practices that you could learn from us (or we could learn from you, for that matter), you have to apply them within the correct formula in your marriage relationship so that they properly account for your unique similarities, differences, tendencies, baggage, strengths, weaknesses, experiences, and goals.

Your P.I.E. still needs a PI. There are too many variables involved for you to directly emulate someone else's marriage. But you can pull out the PI, which is the part of the formula that accounts for differences in your relationship, and apply them in your own unique formula to achieve a powerful marriage where there's nothing missing and nothing broken.

The P.I.E. & PI Effect

The ingredients in marriage represent something different for each family. The things Newt and I need to make our marriage function are completely different than what you may need for your relationship. Nonetheless, each of us has what I like to call, a formula. That formula is the perfect blend of simple ingredients that will give your marriage a wonderful flavor. For example, when my grandmother made her delicious apple pies, she uses the basic ingredients of apples, cinnamon, sugar, flour, salt, butter, nutmeg, and lemon. If you ask any chef, they would agree that these simple ingredients could create a delicious dessert. If these same ingredients were placed in the hands of several different cooks, the apple pies they create would vary in consistency and flavor. My point is uniqueness occurs by the hand, vision, and palate of the cook.

God ordains marriages, and each union is unique and different. Marriage does not have a "one size fits all" formula that works for every relationship. Instead, it takes a specific blend of maturity and sacrifice that work together, and like a fine wine are developed over time.

When you and your spouse begin to build your lives together, there will be a plethora of pleasant discussions along with not-so-pleasant disagreements. Some conversations will be upsetting, and some will be enjoyable. However, both are opportunities for communication and will yield information about your spouse's needs and dislikes. That information will prove powerful as you use it to determine the right blend for your marriage formula. Another thing to remember is that each of you have your own personalities along with independent desires. You'll also have outside activities and/or relationships that are established at work, school or leisure time that you may, or may not spend with your spouse. Ensuring that there's time for these activities are necessary things to include when creating the best formula for your marriage. It's extremely important to communicate, negotiate and be considerate about what each of you need. The amount of time needed will vary and depend upon your personalities, needs, desires, work schedules, family dynamic, and overall goals. Newt and I still negotiate our schedules so that we maintain a well-balanced, healthy relationship. This negotiation process happens weekly and provides us time to discuss our plans for work, exercise activities, and our free-time schedules. Sometimes negotiations are simple, and other times it's like a boardroom discussion that has to be tabled until we think about how or what we can do to modify our plans for the greater good of our marriage.

God ordains marriages, and each union is unique and different. Marriage does not have a "one size fits all" formula that works for every relationship. Instead, it takes a specific blend of maturity and sacrifice that work together, and, like fine wine, are developed over time. Marriage works - and it *is* work; but if you work it, it will work for you! As you grow together, keep in mind that you will never completely master your mate. As each day progresses with new experiences and expectations, you will learn more about yourself and your spouse. It is this continuous learning process that fuels your marriage and catapults you toward accomplishing your visions and aspirations. Your search to know your spouse will be an everlasting discovery of excitement and adventure full of research, soul searching and spiritual connections. So, enjoy the journey because mastery will never be realized.

We started the book by stating that marriage is simple as P.I.E. We know that sustaining a happy and healthy marriage for a lifetime requires an intentional effort. However, we submit that it is not the marriage itself that requires the bulk of that effort; it is us as individuals. Stay hopeful and be encouraged! It is not unrealistic for you to reach a point where you can function together as a single unit and enjoy the bliss of the greatest relationship known to mankind. We believe the secret lies in ensuring these three ingredients are included in the mix that creates the formula for your marriage.

PROVIDE vision and support for one another in all of the things you are building together.

INVEST in one another, both individually and collectively with your time, talent, resources, and love.

Most importantly, **EMPOWER** one another to pursue and maximize your individual purposes so your collective purpose can be more productive and fulfilling.

Threading these three strategies throughout the very fiber of your relationship will make marriage as **"Simple as P. I. E."**

Post – Assess Your Marriage – Chapter 12

To maintain a healthy marriage, you must commit to always *Provide for, Invest* in, and *Empower* one another. Although those ingredients may look and operate differently in each relationship, they are consistent in the recipe of a happy and healthy marriage. The "Assess Your Marriage" activity is designed to help you analyze your relationship and evaluate each of its components so you can be more deliberate in creating a game plan to improve things.

This copy of the "Assess Your Marriage" tool is for you to take *AFTER* reading this book and reflecting upon the content in each chapter. Once you complete the tool on your own, schedule some time with your spouse to compare and contrast each other's assessments and include in the discussion of your assessment with your spouse a comparison between your pre and post version scores. Remember, don't be alarmed when your perception and your spouse's perceptions are different. More than likely, they will be. This is an opportunity to talk to one another, listen to one another, ask questions, and get a better understanding of each other's thoughts and feelings. Approach this exercise as a learner. Don't look now, but the work of building a better marriage is well underway.

To create a culture of continuous improvement in your marriage, complete and compare another post version of the tool at the three-month, six-month, and twelve-month marks. This will provide you with some data you can use to track how much your thinking has changed and how far your relationship has progressed. Most importantly, make sure you keep the conversation going.

Rate each category on a scale of 1-10 *(10 the greatest 1 the lowest).*
Provide a brief reason for the score).

Category	Score	Reason
Goals / Drive/ Aspirations *(Is there a sense that there is a common target or mission that you are accomplishing together?)*		
Sex & Intimacy *(How compatible are your sex drives, definitions of intimacy, and priority levels when it comes to sex and intimacy?)*		
Parenting/ Family Values *(Consider whether your similarities and differences around family values and parenting complement each other or clash. Are they effective or damaging?)*		

Dealing with Conflict

(Consider how you resolve conflict in your marriage. Do you feel you have a good understanding of how and when to address issues in your relationship?)

Career & Money

(How compatible are you in your style of handling money and prioritizing career?)

Household Responsibilities

(Are you happy with your household responsibilities?)

Communication

(Do you feel like you try your best to understand each other's views, feelings, and opinions?)

Faith / Spirituality / Beliefs

(How spiritually compatible are you? Do you assist in each's spiritual growth?)

Friendship with Each Other

(Is your spouse your best friend?)

Managing External Friendships

(Are external relationships prioritized such that they are a help and not a hinderance to your marriage?)

Add the scores for each category to calculate your **Total Score**

Divide the Total Score by 10 to calculate the Average Score of Your Marriage. *(Total Score /10)*

About The Authors

Kimberly H. Miller is a life-learner who is excited about the move of God in this season. She is a simplistic person who sees abundant life as a state of being and not a tangible measurement. Kim believes that each day is a school of change, and she sits in the classroom on the front row, watching God orchestrate and listening to the message of direction. She believes that God wrote the purpose of our lives in our hearts, but life's clutter has blocked area's that we must search deeply to recover. Kimberly believes that this search is her calling to help God's people discover the hidden treasures in their hearts. She has lived out that purpose by mentoring and motivating countless young people, parents, and families through the schools, and the churches and community-based organization to which she has partnered.

Dr. Newton H. Miller II has committed over 25 years of his life to the education arena by serving as a middle school and high school mathematics and science teacher and a principal of both middle and high schools in low performing urban school districts. He has written plans to establish and expand alternative learning settings for disruptive students, helped create and teach remedial math programs on the community college level, consulted in several alternative high schools across the country, and now serves as a professor of education, where he leads a team that builds teacher preparation programs focusing on preparing effective educators to serve all students, but particularly urban and at-risk learners.

Dr. Miller's passion is to help others visualize and activate themselves to call forth their own potential to fulfill their purpose in life. Thus, his mantra and ulterior motive is always to *educate, motivate, and help them grow.* After facing many challenges, roadblocks, and self-dug pitfalls which he had to conquer and overcome in his own life, Dr. Miller has dedicated his research and professional practices to finding what works in educating non-traditional and at-potential populations beginning with strong and healthy families cultures.

Dr. Miller has been a long-time advocate and supporter of strong families and marriages. He has worked to use education to reverse the cycles of perpetuated dysfunction by dismantling and rebuilding a healthy culture around home – school – community relations. Throughout the years, he has been active in local ministries focusing on educating and empowering young people (young men in particular) by encouraging and supporting educational attainment, emphasizing vision, purpose, and self-esteem, and healthy marriage relationships.

Dr. Miller's favorite saying is... "Stay Anxious to Make a Difference!"

Exciting Books by Kim and Dr. Newt

Marriage Books

Marriage Simple as P.I.E. - *Baggage Claim* 1st Edition

Kimberly & Dr. Newton Miller II

Kimberly and Newton are very transparent as they share experiences from their own marriage to provide examples that help readers not only see the importance of unpacking the baggage of the past to maintain a healthy relationship, but how to walk through the unpacking process.

Parenting/Mentoring

Why Some Seeds Don't Grow

Dr. Newton Miller

Why Some Seeds Don't Grow, explores ten principles that will help those who mentor, parent, and educate urban youth develop the mindset needed to help those seeds grow, maximize their potential, and accomplish their purpose.

Author Instructor Course

The Published Author: The instructor Course
Kimberly Miller

Step-by-step instructor course for writing and publishing your own book.

Spiritual Seasons Journal Series

Spiritual Seasons Journal: Fall
Kimberly Miller

Fall is the "letting go to grow season." Fall is unique; everything changes, including the colors of your world. Take time to journal as you watch yourself grow beyond your understanding because when we enter into the season of Fall, we will see ourselves fully bloom in due season.

Spiritual Seasons Journal: Spring
Kimberly Miller

Spring is the season that everything leaps into action. It's the season to maintain and manage the crop. Take time to journal as you watch yourself grow beyond your understanding because when we enter into the season of Spring, we will see ourselves fully bloom in due season.

Spiritual Seasons Journal: Winter
Kimberly Miller

Winter is the winning season. This season you will need to prepare for great growth under the surface and take time to journal as you watch yourself grow beyond your understanding. Don't be fooled by cold or dark days in your Winter because there is a win in Winter.

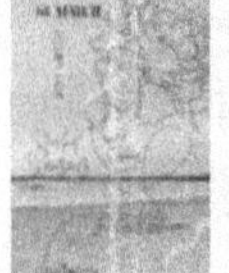

Spiritual Seasons Journal: Summer
Kimberly Miller

Summer is the season of strength. This season, you will need to be ready for all the growth occurring around and in you. Take time to journal as you watch yourself grow beyond your understanding. Because when we understand the seasons of our lives, we will fully bloom in due season.

Children's Books & Activities

Candy Kenya
Kimberly Miller

Candy Kenya presents an easy way to teach children the importance of making good choices and following directions. Children will be reminded of the love that Mommy & Daddy have for them even when it seems like they're just being bossy!

Little Cub
Kimberly Miller

Kids love animals, and learning about them is always fun. This cute little book about Brown bear cubs will help children learn interesting facts about the brown bear. Students will also complete fun activities that support the topic. As a teacher, another way to enjoy this activity book is to copy the activity sheets and coloring pages for students to color, write and discuss. Target ages 0-6

The Potential in You
Kimberly Miller

Teaching children that they have potential and the ability to achieve great things! Target age 1-6

Whoo's Owl
Kimberly Miller

Kids love animals, and learning about them is always fun. This cute little book about Owls will help children learn interesting facts about the adorable Owl animal. Students will also complete fun activities that support mastery of the topic. As a teacher, another way to enjoy this activity book is to copy the activity sheets and coloring pages for students to color and discuss. Target ages 0-6

Launch Kids Forgiveness & Repentance Sunday School Series
Kimberly Miller

In this series, children will learn that God's definition of forgiveness means to pardon or excuse; no longer blame or be angry with someone who has done something wrong. Children will also understand that repentance means to turn away from sin, be sorry for your choices, and make new positive choices.

Who Made it ALL?
Kimberly Miller

Children will see the beauty and complexity of the world while learning about landforms, clouds, and volcanoes. They will also understand and acknowledge that someone greater than themselves created everything.

My Little Hands:
Kimberly Miller

Mi'Kayla is a happy little girl, learning that it takes time to grow. She uses her imagination and heart to touch things that she physically can't reach. In this cute little picture book, students will use their imagination to touch the world. They will also gain an understanding of the contractions used in the story.

Animalbet'z Letter A Animals
Kimberly Miller

Kids love animals, and learning about them is always fun. This cute little Animalbet'z book begins with the letter A, animals. Children will learn interesting facts about adorable animals and complete fun activities that support mastery of the topic. Another way to enjoy this activity book is to copy the activity sheets and coloring pages for kids to color. Target age 1st-5th grade

When Cheerleaders Go on STRIKE!
Kimberly Miller

Children love sports and fun activities, but sometimes those activities are measured against others and minimized for what seems popular. In this funny book, learn how Akai, her cheerleading friends, and Coach Jones teach the football team a valuable lesson about the importance of cheerleaders. Target age 3rd-5th grade

Growing in Circles

Kimberly Miller

Shapes make up many things in our world, and circles are one of the most used shapes. A circle is a curved line that meets at the being of the curve. Circles have no breaks or openings, and it is used to make many cool designs, complete other 3D shapes, and for many of the things you use in your home. Check out all the cool ways that you and I are growing in circles.

Dude Journals

Kimberly Miller

This journal is a guide to help us set goals, declare affirmations, and remind us of our importance and value in the world. When we understand who we are, they will show up in the world as strong, purposeful leaders. I'm Troy, and I'm Zion from Ommy'z World Kids, and it's time to journal about your future.

Teen Journal

Kimberly Miller

Growing up can be challenging. Teenagers deal with puberty and all kinds of physical changes. When puberty knocks on our door, life feels a little more difficult and confusing than usual. We, Teens, need a tool to help us express our feelings and deal with our emotions. So spending time journaling can be a positive outlet to reflect upon our daily experiences. This journal is a guide that will help kids set goals, declare affirmations, and remind us of our importance and value. And most importantly, get us on the path to self-discovery. I'm Jada, and I'm Kimani from Ommy'z World Kids, and it's time to journal about your future.

Tory Too Little

Kimberly Miller

This adorable picture book about Tory presents an easy way to teach children the importance of kindness. Children learn that patience and love are keys to growing up and establishing great friendships!

Jayanni's Letter

Kimberly Miller

Jayanni's Letter is a sweet fictional story about a little girl and the loving relationship between her and her grandmother, Abuela. Each day Jayanni reads a beautiful letter from her grandmother that reassures how much she is loved. However, overtime Jayanni is forced to deal with the unfortunate loss of her Abuela. Thankfully Jayanni had special memories of the letters of love written by her Abuela/grandmother that helped her get through her grief and eventually turn the painful situation into a tradition of letter writing.

Zion Lion King of the Jungle

Kimberly Miller

Zion the Lion is a Realistic-Fiction text about a lion who protects the Pride. Zion is a proud Lion who knows the importance of defending and protecting his family and the Jungle that he maintains. Students will enjoy reading the adventures of Zion while learning essential facts about lions. At the end of the story, you will find Lion facts and activities for students to enjoy and educators to implement in the classroom.

Made to Be King
Kimberly Miller

Newt and his dad travel to the Zoo to learn about Elephants. Newt learns that Elephants are the largest land Mammal, and he believes that the Elephant should be King of the Jungle! While talking to the Elephants, Newt realizes that the Elephant, like humans, can be afraid to face their fears.

Kimya the Hyena Hunter
Kimberly Miller

Kimya, the Hyena Hunter, is a Non-Fictional text told by a fictional character. Kimya takes you on a safari adventure to the heights of mountains, the terrain of forest, the fields of grasslands, and the sands of deserts to find the unique mammal the Spotted Hyena.
So come along and grab your hat, camera, and canteen and, most importantly, your imagination, and let's take an inquisitive journey from continent to continent and learn more about the Spotted Hyena.

That's Why I Dance: Layla's Praise

Kimberly Miller

That's Why I Dance: Layla's Praise is about a brilliant and energetic little girl with a vivid imagination who loves to worship through dance. Read how Layla expresses her heart through liturgical dance while inspiring the reader to work hard at achieving their dreams.

For a complete list of our titles and to request signed copies of this book and other titles written by Kim and Dr. Newt visit us at www.newEDproducts.net

Get your Baggage Claim workbook

www.newedproducts.net/shop

Launch 360 Marriage Ministries

Inquire about our customized marriage seminars or marriage information sessions (in-person or virtual) where we build a program to meet your specific needs. Contact us at directly: msap@drnewt2.com